NORMAN SCHWARZKOPF

U.S. ARM
SCHWARZKOPF

THE CHELSEA HOUSE LIBRARY OF BIOGRAPHY

NORMAN SCHWARZKOPF

REBECCA STEFOFF

Chelsea House Publishers

CHELSEA HOUSE PUBLISHERS

Editor-in-Chief Remmel Nunn
Managing Editor Karyn Gullen Browne
Copy Chief Mark Rifkin
Picture Editor Adrian Allen
Art Director Maria Epes
Assistant Art Director Howard Brotman
Manufacturing Director Gerald Levine
Systems Manager Lindsey Ottman
Production Manager Joseph Romano
Production Coordinator Marie Claire Cebrián

The Chelsea House Library of Biography
Senior Editor Kathy Kuhtz

Staff for ***NORMAN SCHWARZKOPF***
Associate Editor Scott Prentzas
Copy Editor Ian Wilker
Editorial Assistant Tamar Levovitz
Picture Researcher Wendy P. Wills
Senior Designer Basia Niemczyc
Cover Illustration Alan Nahigian

Printed and bound in Mexico.

3 5 7 9 8 6 4 2

Library of Congress Cataloging-in-Publication Data

Stefoff, Rebecca
Norman Schwarzkopf/Rebecca Stefoff.
p. cm.—(The Chelsea House library of biography)
Includes bibliographical references and index.
Summary: A biography of the popular military leader, tracing his rise through the ranks of the army and his role as commander of the U.S. troops in the Persian Gulf.
ISBN 0-7910-1725-7
0-7910-1726-5 (pbk.)
1. Schwarzkopf, H. Norman, 1934—Juvenile literature. 2. Generals—United States—Biography—Juvenile literature. 3. United States. Army—Biography—Juvenile Literature. [1. Schwarzkopf, H. Norman, 1934– 2. Generals.] I. Title. II. Series.
E840.5.S39S74 1992 91-23325
355'.0092—dc20 CIP
[B] AC

Contents

THE CHELSEA HOUSE LIBRARY OF BIOGRAPHY

Barbara Bush

John C. Calhoun

Clarence Darrow

Charles Darwin

Anne Frank

William Lloyd Garrison

Raisa Gorbachev

Martha Graham

J. Edgar Hoover

Saddam Hussein

Jesse James

Rose Kennedy

John Lennon

Jack London

Horace Mann

Edward R. Murrow

William Penn

Edgar Allan Poe

Norman Schwarzkopf

Joseph Smith

Sam Walton

Frank Lloyd Wright

Boris Yeltsin

Brigham Young

Other titles in the series are forthcoming.

Introduction

Learning from Biographies

Vito Perrone

The oldest narratives that exist are biographical. Much of what we know, for example, about the Pharaohs of ancient Egypt, the builders of Babylon, the philosophers of Greece, the rulers of Rome, the many biblical and religious leaders who provide the base for contemporary spiritual beliefs, has come to us through biographies—the stories of their lives. Although an oral tradition was long the mainstay of historically important biographical accounts, the oral stories making up this tradition became by the 1st century A.D. central elements of a growing written literature.

In the 1st century A.D., biography assumed a more formal quality through the work of such writers as Plutarch, who left us more than 500 biographies of political and intellectual leaders of Rome and Greece. This tradition of focusing on great personages lasted well into the 20th century and is seen as an important means of understanding the history of various times and places. We learn much, for example, from Plutarch's writing about the collapse of the Greek city-states and about the struggles in Rome over the justice and the constitutionality of a world empire. We also gain considerable understanding of the definitions of morality and civic virtue and how various common men and women lived out their daily existence.

Not surprisingly, the earliest American writing, beginning in the 17th century, was heavily biographical. Those Europeans who came to America were dedicated to recording their experience, especially the struggles they faced in building what they determined to be a new culture. John Norton's *Life and Death of John Cotton*, printed in 1630, typifies these early works. Later biographers often tackled more ambitious projects. Cotton Mather's *Magnalia Christi Americana*, published in 1702, accounted for the lives of more than 70 ministers and political leaders. In addition, a biographical literature around the theme of Indian captivity had considerable popularity. Soon after the American Revolution and the organization of the United States of America, Americans were treated to a large outpouring of biographies about such figures as Benjamin Franklin, George Washington, Thomas Jefferson, and Aaron Burr, among others. These particular works served to build a strong sense of national identity.

Among the diverse forms of historical literature, biographies have been over many centuries the most popular. And in recent years interest in biography has grown even greater, as biography has gone beyond prominent government figures, military leaders, giants of business, industry, literature, and the arts. Today we are treated increasingly to biographies of more common people who have inspired others by their particular acts of courage, by their positions on important social and political issues, or by their dedicated lives as teachers, town physicians, mothers, and fathers. Through this broader biographical literature, much of which is featured in THE CHELSEA HOUSE LIBRARY OF BIOGRAPHY, our historical understandings can be enriched greatly.

What makes biography so compelling? Most important, biography is a human story. In this regard, it makes of history something personal, a narrative with which we can make an intimate connection. Biographers typically ask us as readers to accompany them on a journey through the life of another person, to see some part of the world through another's eyes. We can, as a result, come to understand what it is like to live the life of a slave, a farmer, a textile worker, an engineer, a poet, a president—in a sense, to walk in another's shoes. Such experience can be personally invaluable. We cannot ask for a better entry into historical studies.

Although our personal lives are likely not as full as those we are reading about, there will be in most biographical accounts many common experiences. As with the principal character of any biography, we are also faced with numerous decisions, large and small. In the midst of living our lives we are not usually able to comprehend easily the significance of our daily decisions or grasp easily their many possible consequences, but we can gain important insights into them by seeing the decisions made by others play themselves out. We can learn from others.

Because biography is a personal story, it is almost always full of surprises. So often, the personal lives of individuals we come across historically are out of view, their public personas masking who they are. It is through biography that we gain access to their private lives, to the acts that define who they are and what they truly care about. We see their struggles within the possibilities and limitations of life, gaining insight into their beliefs, the ways they survived hardships, what motivated them, and what discouraged them. In the process we can come to understand better our own struggles.

As you read this biography, try to place yourself within the subject's world. See the events as that person sees them. Try to understand why the individual made particular decisions and not others. Ask yourself if you would have chosen differently. What are the values or beliefs that guide the subject's actions? How are those values or beliefs similar to yours? How are they different from yours? Above all, remember: You are engaging in an important historical inquiry as you read a biography, but you are also reading a literature that raises important personal questions for you to consider.

While on patrol in February 1968, infantrymen from the Americal Division cautiously walk through a rice paddy near Nghi Hai, South Vietnam. Lt. Colonel Norman Schwarzkopf served as a battalion commander in the Americal Division from December 1969 to July 1970.

1

A Minefield in Batangan

MIDWAY ALONG THE EAST COAST OF VIETNAM, a small patch of land called the Batangan Peninsula juts into the warm waters of the South China Sea. Batangan is flat and green, covered with jungle and rice paddies, threaded with silty brown streams, and fringed with mangrove swamps where the land meets the sea. Tucked between the coastal town of Quang Ngai to the south and the more important city of Da Nang to the north, Batangan today is a placid, densely populated backwater. But in 1970, when the Vietnam War was raging across Southeast Asia, it was a bloody battleground.

Troops from the United States fought in many parts of Vietnam, but some of the most intense fighting took place along the central coast. Although the area belonged to South Vietnam, an ally of the United States, most of the villagers and peasants were sympathetic to the National Liberation Front (NLF), a group of Communist and nationalist rebels. NLF guerrillas—called the Vietcong (Vietnamese Communists) by the South Vietnamese government—and soldiers from Communist North Vietnam were therefore able to infiltrate the region and lay in ambush for American and South Vietnamese troops. They also laid thousands of mines—bomblike devices buried just beneath the surface of the ground and set to explode with devastating effect when someone stepped on or near them. By early 1970, the Americal Division, the U.S. Infantry unit based at Chu Lai, just north of Batangan, had lost more than three-fourths of its casualties not to combat but to booby traps and hidden explosives. The commanding officers of the Americal Division had come to think of Batangan as one enormous minefield.

On May 28, one of those commanding officers was riding above Batangan in a Huey helicopter. He was a 35-year-old lieutenant colonel named H. Norman Schwarzkopf, and he headed an infantry battalion in the Americal Division. His troops were conducting a sweep of the terrain below, searching for concealed enemies, while he monitored their progress via radio reports from company commanders on the ground. Next to him sat Captain Robert Trabbert, a lower-ranking artillery officer who was helping Schwarzkopf coordinate the operation.

With a crackle of static, a sudden announcement came over the radio. One of Schwarzkopf's troop companies—Bravo Company—was in trouble. Some of the men had entered a minefield, setting off the buried explosives. The company commander and his lieutenant were badly wounded. A medevac unit, as the medical evacuation helicopters were called, was on its way to the scene to rescue the injured officers. But the rest of the soldiers were frozen in place, afraid to move because the next step might detonate another mine. And while they waited there, they were at risk of being sighted and shot at by a Vietcong patrol.

Lieutenant Colonel Schwarzkopf got the coordinates of the minefield from the radio operator and ordered his pilot to fly to the site. His Huey reached the minefield before the medevac chopper arrived, so he and Trabbert got out

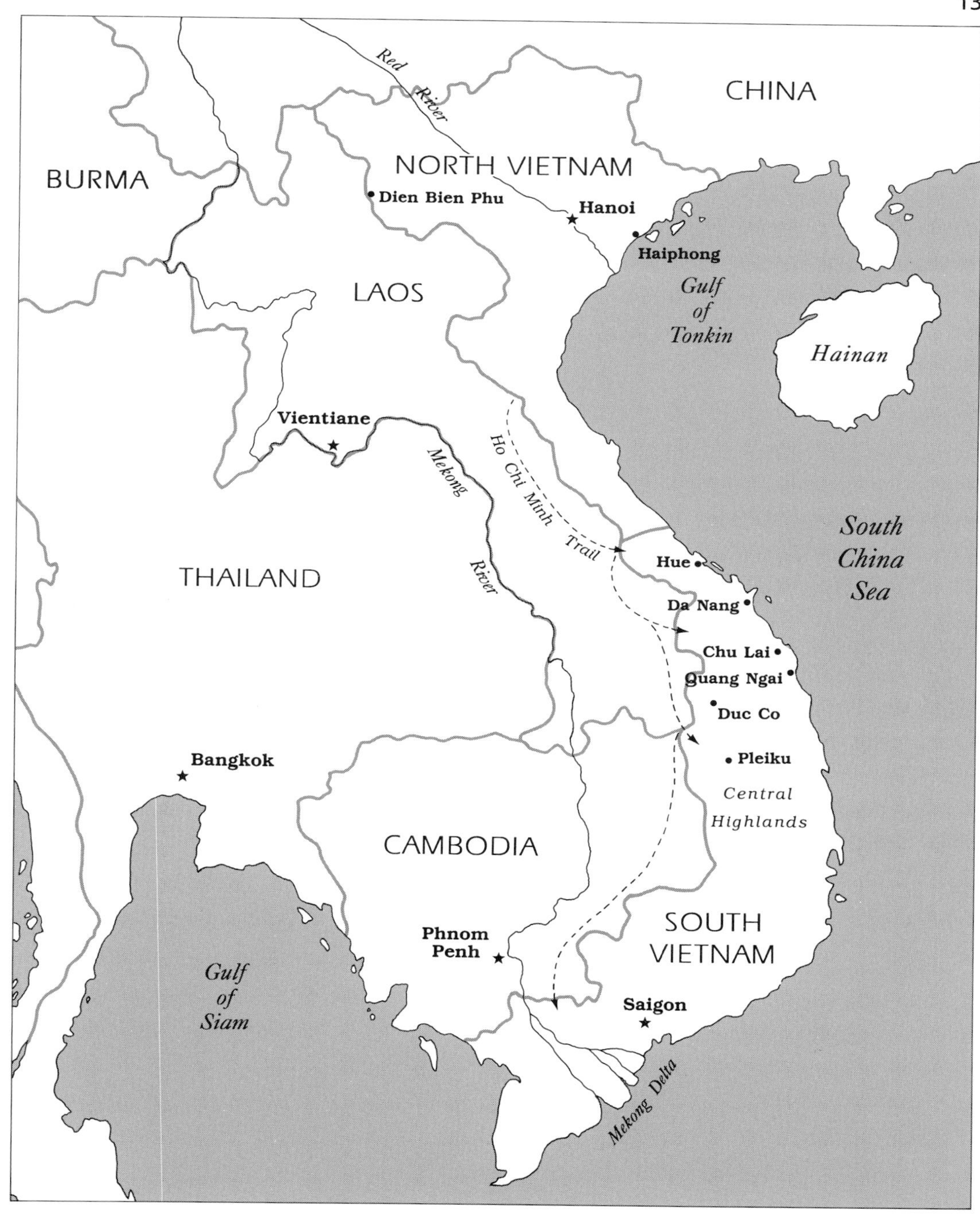

Southeast Asia During the Vietnam War

A U.S. Army helicopter lands on an open patch of land during an intense firefight between American troops and the Vietcong. Throughout its involvement in combat during the Vietnam War (1965–73), the army used helicopters as gunboats, troop transports, and ambulances.

and sent the wounded officers back to the base in their Huey. Schwarzkopf and Trabbert stayed behind with Bravo Company.

Schwarzkopf knew that fear was Bravo Company's biggest enemy just then. The soldiers were young and scared. They had seen their leaders blown up in front of them. Now their nerves were stretched to the limit, and they were on the edge of panic. At any moment they might bolt for cover, which would almost certainly set off more mines. Schwarzkopf was their commanding officer—he had to keep them calm and try to get them out of the minefield alive.

"Okay, we're going to get you out of here," Schwarzkopf told them. He went on to issue instructions in a steady voice: "Slowly, now, I want you to walk back out of the field the way you went in. Watch where you put your feet, keep to your old tracks. Stay calm, keep your distance."

The men turned and slowly began to inch their way back toward Schwarzkopf. Then a private about 30 or 40 feet from the lieutenant colonel stepped on a mine. The explosion threw the young man into the air and tore at his leg. Schwarzkopf and Trabbert felt the shock wave and were sprayed with dirt and sharp bits of shrapnel. When the private hit the ground, his broken leg was twisted to one side.

"My leg!" he screamed in shock and terror. "My leg!"

Schwarzkopf told Trabbert to get on the radio and tell the medevac unit to hurry. He glanced at the rest of the men. They stood white-faced and petrified. The injured soldier was writhing and hitting the ground in pain, and Schwarzkopf could see reflected in the other men's eyes the dreadful fear that his thrashing might set off still another mine. For his own sake and everyone else's, the injured private had to be immobilized.

Very carefully, placing one foot slowly ahead of the other, Schwarzkopf stepped into the minefield, working his way toward the man on the ground. He was still 20 feet away when the fallen soldier began to scream again. "I'm going to die!" he wailed. "We're all going to die!"

Schwarzkopf paused. Sweat dripped into his eyes. His legs were shaking, and he had to grab his knees to hold them steady while he took a deep breath. The frightened soldiers all around were staring anxiously at him, waiting to see what he would do. At that moment, he later recalled, he thought of the sign that President Harry Truman had placed on his own desk in the White House: The Buck Stops Here. There was no one else to do the job. The only thing to do was to go on.

The injured private was crying, saying, "You've got to get me out of here." As he stepped forward again, Schwarzkopf said, "I'll get you out. You're going to be okay." A few moments later he reached the wounded soldier. Schwarzkopf gently lowered his own six-foot three-inch frame over the young man's body to hold him still. Everyone began to breathe again. Nothing had exploded.

The next step was to set the broken leg. Schwarzkopf called to Trabbert to find a splint. Trabbert handed his knife to a soldier who was standing near a small tree and told him to cut a branch to serve as a splint. When the soldier stepped toward the tree, he triggered a mine. The explosion killed the soldier with the knife and two others instantly. Trabbert, too, absorbed some of the blast. Shrapnel blew off his left leg, shattered one of his elbows, and punched a hole in his head. The medevac team arrived in time, however, and he lived. Schwarzkopf, the wounded private, and the other soldiers in Bravo Company were also evacuated from the minefield.

The army rewarded Lieutenant Colonel Schwarzkopf with a Silver Star in recognition of the valor he showed in entering the minefield to save the wounded private. But to Schwarzkopf, the episode was nothing special; he was simply doing his duty. He knew that it was his responsibility to take care of the men in his command. He also

The U.S. Army awards the Silver Star to recognize bravery in combat. In 1970, Schwarzkopf received his third Silver Star for entering a minefield to save a wounded soldier.

knew that by doing his duty—by entering the minefield to calm the injured soldier—he had escaped death or injury himself. If he had not been in the minefield with the soldier, he would have been standing next to Trabbert when the second mine went off. The quirk of fate that had saved him and mangled Trabbert was, he understood, one of the bitter ironies of war. "You live with those things," he said. "You become terribly fatalistic in combat."

Other things about Norman Schwarzkopf's Vietnam experience, however, were harder for him to live with and understand. He recounted the incident of the Batangan minefield to journalist and author C. D. B. Bryan, and it was also to Bryan that he confessed, a few months after he left Vietnam, that he was deeply disturbed by the way the Vietnam War had divided the American people. Through the course of the war, the antiwar movement had grown stronger in the United States. Doubts about the rightness of the war and the way it was being fought became more widespread, and segments of the U.S. public loudly voiced their disapproval of the military in protest marches and demonstrations. By the time Schwarzkopf returned to the United States, soldiers were being spat upon and greeted with shouts of "baby-killer!" and other epithets.

On February 24, 1991, Schwarzkopf holds a press briefing 10 hours after the beginning of the ground war in Operation Desert Storm. The U.S. general led the forces of the United States and its allies in their successful mission to oust Iraqi troops from Kuwait.

"I *hate* what Vietnam has done to our country! I *hate* what Vietnam has done to our Army!" Schwarzkopf exclaimed to Bryan. He thought about leaving the army. In the end, however, he decided to stay. It was a decision that, 20 years later, was to have profound consequences for the United States, the Middle East, and the entire world.

Schwarzkopf would remain in the army, rising through the ranks, doing his duty as he saw it, and working in whatever way he could to restore public faith in the armed forces. He would become the model military officer—hardworking, ready to move his family across the country or around the world each time he received new orders, filled with a strong sense of duty and service. Yet Norman Schwarzkopf was never just a textbook general or a cog in the gears of the military machine. His every action demonstrated his character and values, his determination, intelligence, and compassion. He was a most unusual general: a fighting man who hated war, a loyal soldier who was not afraid to think independently and speak his mind. Both his hot temper and his good humor seemed larger than life; together they earned him the nickname Bear—part grizzly bear, part teddy bear.

In 1990, 20 years after Norman Schwarzkopf considered leaving the U.S. Army, the Persian Gulf nation of Iraq invaded its tiny neighbor, the oil-rich nation of Kuwait. As Kuwait's ally, the United States went to war against Iraq in the Persian Gulf. Norman Schwarzkopf, who had risen to the rank of four-star general, was the commander of the U.S. forces in the Persian Gulf, heading the largest American field force since World War II (1939–45). Through his actions in Operation Desert Storm, as the U.S. war effort was called, he has done more than any other individual to put the ghosts of Vietnam to rest. Twenty years after the jungles of Vietnam, he led the air and ground troops of the United States and its allies to victory over Iraq in the deserts of the Middle East. During eight months in the field and six weeks of fighting, he earned a new nickname, "Stormin' Norman" Schwarzkopf, and became the most celebrated military leader of his generation.

Military experts praise Schwarzkopf's leadership in the war and claim that his elegant, decisive battle plans will be studied by historians and strategists in future generations. To the ordinary people of the United States, however, he was more than simply a victorious general. A symbol of plainspoken, hard-hitting American competence, he became an icon; his name and face quickly appeared on bumper stickers, T-shirts, and other merchandise. He represented both strength and integrity and became a source of renewed national pride for many people. During and after Operation Desert Storm, H. Norman Schwarzkopf was a hero—America's first military hero in decades.

Herbert Norman Schwarzkopf, Sr., served as the first superintendent of the New Jersey State Police. Schwarzkopf, who rose to the rank of brigadier general in the U.S. Army, inspired his son to pursue a military career.

2

Son of a Soldier

EVERYTHING IN H. NORMAN SCHWARZKOPF'S LIFE, even his family background, seems to have pointed him toward a military destiny. His father, H. Norman Schwarzkopf, Sr., was an army officer who made it clear that he hoped his son would follow in his footsteps and become a military man. In many ways, the younger Schwarzkopf's life and career echo those of his father.

Christian Schwarzkopf, the grandfather of Schwarzkopf, Jr., was a German jeweler who came to the United States in 1852. Christian Schwarzkopf's wife was also a German immigrant, and they spoke only German in their home. In 1917, their son Herbert Norman Schwarzkopf graduated from the U.S. Military Academy at West Point, New York. The academy at West Point provides the U.S. Army with nearly all of its officers, and in 1917 the army had need of new officers—the United States was embroiled in World War I (1914–18), which pitted Germany and its allies against France, the United Kingdom, and the United States

Ruth Ann Schwarzkopf, Norman's mother

on the battlefields of Europe. Herbert Norman Schwarzkopf was sent to the front lines in early 1918. He was injured in an attack in which the Germans discharged mustard gas, a poisonous substance used in chemical warfare.

The war ended in the fall of 1918. Because he spoke German, Schwarzkopf was put in charge of U.S. Army efforts to rebuild several villages in the German countryside. He was promoted to the rank of colonel. In 1920, however, he left the army and returned to the family home in New Jersey to be near his father, who had become ill. He went to work in a department store in Newark, New Jersey, but in 1921 he was called away from that job to take on a challenging new assignment. The state of New Jersey had decided to organize its first state police force, and Colonel Herbert Norman Schwarzkopf, who was 25 years old at the time, was chosen as its first superintendent. As superintendent, Schwarzkopf was responsible for recruiting and training the men who would become New Jersey's first state troopers. He chose 81 troopers from 1,600 applicants and then set about making them into a paramilitary force. Schwarzkopf possessed first-rate soldierly skills—for example, he was a sure shot with a pistol—and he expected excellence in all things from his troopers. Those who served under him remember that he liked to surprise rookie troopers with such sudden, difficult questions as "What five qualities impress you most about a horse?"

In November 1929, Schwarzkopf, still superintendent of the New Jersey State Police, married Ruth Ann Bowman, who had been the supervisor of nurses at Mercer Hospital in Trenton, New Jersey. The Schwarzkopfs settled into a house in Pennington, just outside of Trenton. They had two daughters, whom they named Ruth Ann and Sally Joan. Then, in 1932, a national tragedy—the kidnapping of aviator Charles A. Lindbergh's infant son—also became the biggest drama of Schwarzkopf's state police career.

Charles A. Lindbergh was a national hero, probably the best-known pilot in history and the first person to cross an ocean by air. In 1927, in a small plane called *The Spirit of St. Louis*, he made the first nonstop solo transatlantic flight, flying from New York City to Paris, France, and winning a prize of $25,000 and the nickname "Lucky Lindy." Soon afterward he married Anne Morrow, the daughter of a diplomat, and the two settled in the small town of Hopewell in central New Jersey, where they wanted to live quietly, out of the public eye. But on March 1, 1932, their first child, a 20-month-old boy, was kidnapped.

The tragedy at once became the leading news story of the day; newspapers dubbed the kidnapping "The Crime of the Century." Thousands of journalists and curiosity seekers converged on Hopewell from across the nation. Immediately and loudly, the public called on the state police to capture the kidnapper and rescue Charles A. Lindbergh, Jr. (At that time, kidnapping was a state crime and was investigated by state, rather than federal, law-enforcement agencies. Partly as a result of the Lindbergh case, kidnapping was later made a federal crime, to be

On March 9, 1932, H. Norman Schwarzkopf, Sr., updates reporters with information about his investigation into the kidnapping of the infant son of aviator Charles Lindbergh. Schwarzkopf's handling of the case became highly controversial.

handled by the Federal Bureau of Investigation.) With the approval of the governor of New Jersey, Schwarzkopf appointed himself head of the investigation. He vowed to solve the case personally, not knowing that it would be four years before the case was closed. His handling of the case would become highly controversial.

Although the Lindberghs paid the $50,000 that had been demanded in a ransom note, they never saw their son alive again. His murdered body was found in a shallow grave not far from their home. Schwarzkopf and his men were fiercely determined to bring the murderer to justice. In order to shield the grieving Lindberghs from the press and the curiosity seekers, Schwarzkopf set up his headquarters in their garage and took firm control of all information about the case. He kept reporters at a distance and issued only a few public statements. One irate reporter grumbled that the Lindbergh case was shrouded in greater secrecy than troop movements during World War I. For a year and a half after the kidnapping, Schwarzkopf's photo appeared frequently in the nation's newspapers as speculation about the case raged unchecked. Meanwhile, the investigation proceeded down a series of disappointing dead ends.

Then, in September 1934, Schwarzkopf arrested a suspect named Bruno Hauptmann, a German immigrant living in New York City who was found in possession of some of the bills that had been included in the Lindberghs' ransom payment. Hauptmann went to trial, was convicted, and died in the electric chair in 1936. But not everyone believed that he was guilty. From the start, the affair had contained many mysterious and confusing elements, and some people felt that Schwarzkopf, eager to close the case at last, had been too ready to accept Hauptmann as guilty on the basis of circumstantial evidence. It was many years before the Lindbergh kidnapping faded from the headlines, and questions continued to be raised about Schwarzkopf's investigation. When his term as state police superintendent expired, he was not reappointed.

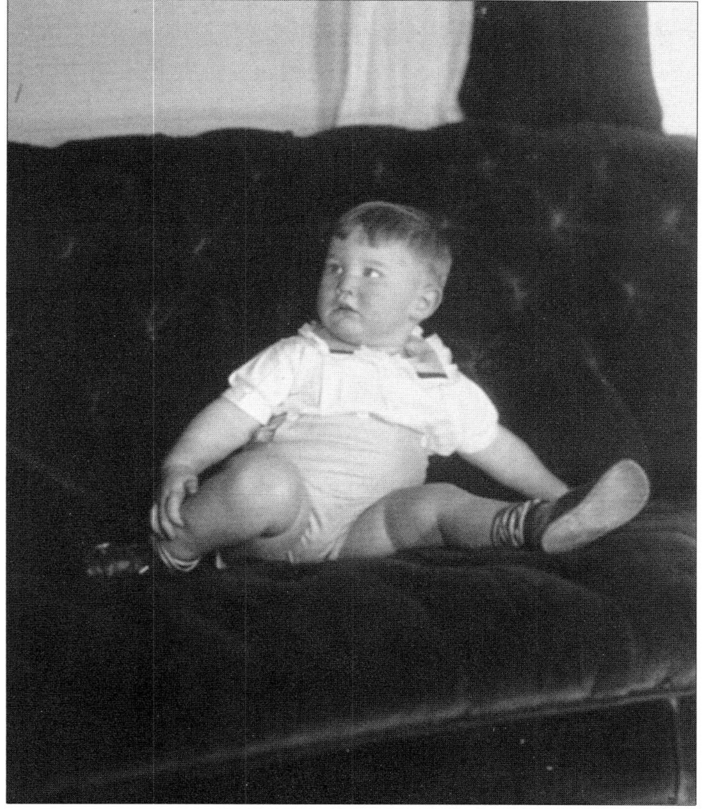

Two-year-old Norman Schwarzkopf plays on a couch at his parents' home. He was born on August 22, 1934, near Trenton, New Jersey.

In the decades since 1936, many books and articles have been written about the Lindbergh kidnapping and the subsequent investigation, and some of these accounts have been critical of Schwarzkopf. Nevertheless, Schwarzkopf remained firmly convinced that Hauptmann was guilty, and the Lindberghs agreed with him.

The young Schwarzkopf children knew little about the case that consumed their father and occupied the nation's headlines during those years. A third child, a boy, had been born on August 22, 1934, just a month before Hauptmann's arrest. Schwarzkopf wanted his son to carry his name—but at the same time he had always hated the name Herbert and did not want to pass it on to the boy. The baby was therefore named H. Norman Schwarzkopf, Jr.; the *H* does not stand

In 1941, seven-year-old Norman joins his sisters Ruth Ann (far right) and Sally (left) and his father outside the family's house in Lawrenceville, New Jersey.

for anything, and Schwarzkopf, Jr., has always been called Norman or Norm.

Soon after Norman's birth, the Schwarzkopf family moved from Pennington to Lawrenceville, a community between Trenton and Princeton, New Jersey. For the first 12 years of Norman's life, the Schwarzkopf family lived in a two-story brick house on Lawrenceville's Main Street. The Schwarzkopfs attended a local Presbyterian church, and when the children were old enough to start school, they rode a bus to the public school in Princeton, five miles from home.

One of Norman's earliest memories is of being allowed to stay up late on Friday nights to hear his father's voice on the radio. On the strength of his nationwide reputation as a lawman, Schwarzkopf had been hired as the host of a radio program called "Gangbusters," a true-crime adventure series. At the end of each program, Schwarzkopf gave the listening audience a clue to an unsolved crime—and on a few occasions these clues led to an arrest.

Norman was an outgoing, active youngster. He and the other boys in the neighborhood played rambunctious games of cowboys and Indians or cops and robbers. His hobby was performing parlor magic, and he became a good amateur magician, mastering coin tricks and card tricks. The interest in magic stayed with him. As an adult, Norman joined the Society of Amateur Magicians, and later he entertained his own children with magic shows. Boyhood friends recall him as protective of his older sisters. He was especially close to Sally, who was closer to his age than Ruth and a bit of a tomboy. He and Sally have remained good friends all their life.

In 1939, when Norman was five years old, World War II broke out in Europe. As a former army officer, the senior Schwarzkopf paid close attention to the news of the war even though the United States was not yet involved. A few years later, however, the war changed the Schwarzkopfs' life. In December 1941, Japan bombed a U.S. naval fleet at Pearl Harbor, Hawaii, and the United States immediately entered the war. Trained military officers were desperately needed. Although he had left the army more than 20 years earlier, Colonel Schwarzkopf was called back to active duty and told that he would be sent overseas. In early 1942, just before he left home, Schwarzkopf handed his heavy West Point sword to seven-year-old Norman and told him, "Now you're the man of the house."

Schwarzkopf was sent to southwest Asia—not to the front lines of a combat zone, as in World War I, but to the Persian Gulf region. His destination was Iran, a country unfamiliar to most Westerners, where the Soviet Union to the north, Asia to the east, and the Arab world to the west meet in a jumble of mountains and desert. Iran was not a theater of war in World War II, but it was the setting of activities crucial to the United States and its allies. The Soviet Union was one of those allies, along with France and the United Kingdom, all united in war against Germany, Italy, and Japan. Iran, located south of the Soviet

Union, was also a U.S. ally, and the United States was able to build a supply route through the mountains of northern Iran to carry food, munitions, and other goods to the Soviet Union.

But Iran was a wild and dangerous place, and the route was beset by mountain bandits who swooped down from their hiding places in the rugged peaks to attack the supply convoys. Iran's military police were unable to control the bandits, so the shah, or ruler, of Iran asked the United States for help in organizing and training a national police force. Schwarzkopf, whose background combined army and state police experience and who was a proven organizer and trainer, was put in charge of the task. Eventually the army promoted him to the rank of brigadier general.

Back home in New Jersey, Schwarzkopf's wife and children waited out the war years. Every week they received a long, rambling letter from Schwarzkopf, 15 or 20 pages describing Iran and its people, culture, art, music, and politics. Sometimes the letters included little sketches of things Schwarzkopf had seen. Every letter ended with personal messages for each member of the family; Norman's message always reminded him to take care of his mother and sisters. These long letters from an exotic, faraway world filled young Norman with excitement. They also reminded him that his father, though absent, still cared deeply for his family. This taught him the importance of communication, and, decades later, when Norman himself was away on duty in the Persian Gulf, he would take care to stay in close touch with his own wife and children.

The war ended in 1945, but Schwarzkopf's work in Iran was not done. The Soviet Union had stationed troops in Iran during the war, and at the end of the war the Soviets refused to withdraw these troops because Joseph Stalin, the Soviet ruler, hoped to win a foothold in oil-rich Iran. The Soviet Union stirred up unrest in the province of Azerbaijan, in northern Iran. Schwarzkopf's national police force, numbering 21,000, was charged with putting down the Azerbaijan rebellion. These international affairs struck close to home when Norman's sister Sally saw a headline in the *Trenton Times* that read SCHWARZKOPF CALLED MURDERER BY SOVIET UNION. The children's mother had to explain to them that the Soviets were wrong and that their father was not a criminal.

Schwarzkopf, Sr., was to remain in Iran until 1948 as the head of a U.S. military mission there. With the fighting over, he decided to send for his family. In 1946 Norman, now 12 years old, flew to Iran. He was overjoyed that he was to join his adored father, and he was also thrilled that he was to see and experience for himself the wonderful things his father had described in his letters.

Norman and his father went on long horseback rides together in the deserts of Iran. Schwarzkopf taught his son to hunt and shoot, activities that became lifelong passions for Norman. The boy picked up a few words in Farsi, the

On December 7, 1941, the USS Arizona *explodes during the Japanese surprise attack on the U.S. naval base at Pearl Harbor, Hawaii. On the following day, the United States declared war on Japan and entered World War II.*

Iranian language. He learned something about Islam, the religion of the Iranian people and their Arab neighbors, and became familiar with some of the customs of the Muslims, or followers of Islam. Later in his own career, this knowledge would help him win the respect of the Muslim rulers and people of Saudi Arabia. Norman also had some experiences that taught him about the open-mindedness one must possess to live successfully among people of another culture. On one occasion his father took him to an Iranian banquet. He was offered a platter of sheep's eyes. A warning glance from his father told him to eat and be polite about it, and young Norman did so. Years later, when he was fighting side by side with local troops in the jungles of Vietnam, he took pride in the fact that, unlike many American officers, he ate what the South Vietnamese soldiers ate, including monkey, snake, and dog meat.

At first, Norman and his father lived in Tehran, the capital of Iran, in a large compound shared by many U.S. military and diplomatic officials. When Norman's mother and sisters arrived in Iran, about six months after his own arrival, the Schwarzkopf family was assigned a private residence—one that happened to be a small palace, with a large staff of servants. A week after they moved in, Schwarzkopf, Sr., called the family together and issued strict instructions. None of the children was to ring a bell or give an order to a servant. He did not want his children to get used to living in a grand setting or to form habits that would be out of place in suburban New Jersey. Nor were the children allowed to miss school. They attended a Presbyterian mission school, the only English-speaking school in Tehran at that time.

In 1947, General Schwarzkopf was transferred to Geneva, Switzerland, and he took his family with him. The children entered an international boarding school. Norman lived in the boys' dorm and shared classes and sports with children from many countries. Tall for his age and strong, he was good at soccer and tennis.

The following year Schwarzkopf, Sr., was transferred to Berlin, Germany, where he served under General Lucius Clay, the military governor of the U.S. sector of the city. After Germany's defeat in the war, its capital city of Berlin had been divided into four zones. Each was administered by one of the victorious Allies—France, the United Kingdom, the United States, and the Soviet Union. Germany's economy had been ravaged by the war, and many goods were in short supply in the postwar years. As a result, smuggling between the different sectors was widespread. Schwarzkopf organized an antismuggling campaign for the U.S. military police in Germany.

Norman started high school in Germany. Then his father was transferred to Rome, to be the head of a U.S. military mission there, and Norman lived in Italy for a time. In the course of more than three years in Europe, Norman grew into a vigorous, ambitious teenager. He played every sport that he could, he joined the student councils at his schools, and he had fun with other young people, many of them the sons of officers like his father. Through his family's travels, he gained a cosmopolitan familiarity with the airports and hotels in several European countries, and he learned quite a bit of German, as well as smatterings of other languages. Norman also became familiar with army life: the intricate details of rank and protocol, the constant transfers, the set routines of army bases the world over. He began to imagine what his own future would be like if he chose the military life.

In 1950 the U.S. Army sent General Schwarzkopf back to Iran. The general's daughters were in college at Smith and Wellesley back in the United States, and he decided that his son should also return to the United States to complete his high school education. This, he felt, would be Norman's best preparation for what lay ahead. For father and son now shared the same ambition: that Norman should follow in his father's footsteps to the U.S. Military Academy at West Point and then on to the U.S. Army.

Norman Schwarzkopf poses for his U.S. Military Academy graduation photograph in 1956. After completing the academy's four-year program, Schwarzkopf received a bachelor of science degree and a commission as a second lieutenant in the U.S. Army.

3

The Making of a Military Man

IT IS IMPOSSIBLE TO DISENTANGLE Norman Schwarzkopf's own plans for his life from the plans that his father had for him. Norman profoundly admired his father and grew up very much in his father's image, sharing the older man's patriotism and sense of duty. "A lot of my love of country stemmed from my father," Norman Schwarzkopf says today. "My dad was a genuine public servant who had a deep and abiding love for his country, and he wanted to serve."

When Norman was four years old, Schwarzkopf, Sr., told him that one day he too would go to West Point and be a soldier. Later, Norman enthusiastically adopted this plan, and he never wavered from it. When he was 10 years old, while his father was in Iran, Norman's parents took him out of public school and enrolled him in the Bordentown Military Academy at Bordentown, New Jersey, not far from home. When the time came to have his class picture taken at the academy, he was told that he could choose between smiling or wearing a serious expression. He adopted a grim, unsmiling look for the photograph. When his mother asked why, he replied, "Later on, when I'm a general, I want them to know I'm serious."

Early in 1950, before his return to Iran, General Schwarzkopf sent an application for his son to the Valley Forge Military Academy in Pennsylvania. Schwarzkopf wrote, "Norman is most anxious to become a cadet at the United States Military Academy. Naturally, I heartily concur in his ambitions." The application was accepted. Schwarzkopf, Sr., headed for Iran, where he spent a year as the security adviser for one of the country's leading political figures, and Schwarzkopf, Jr., headed for Pennsylvania, where he entered Valley Forge at 16 years of age. At the time, he stood 6 feet 2 inches, just an inch short of his adult height, and he weighed more than 200 muscular pounds. He was made starting lineman on the school's football team.

Valley Forge Military Academy, founded in 1928, is located just outside Philadelphia. Its students, called cadets, study standard high school subjects, but they wear uniforms and follow a structured, military-style schedule, waking to the sound of bugle calls and forming ranks for daily inspection. Schwarzkopf was housed in a dormitory called Wheeler Hall; his room overlooked the parade ground where cadets were taught marching drills. He ate with the other cadets in a communal mess hall.

The academy is staffed by men with military backgrounds. During Schwarzkopf's time at the academy, the important post of commandant of cadets was filled by Major General Milton H. Medenbach, a retired army officer who was responsible for disciplining the cadets. Those guilty of misbehaving had to walk "tours" around the parade ground, and Schwarzkopf made a few such tours. One entry on his cadet record reads, "It is hoped that you have had time to think this over and understand that we never throw any article of food in the mess hall at Valley Forge." Medenbach had a high opinion of Schwarzkopf because the young cadet was never content simply to get by; instead, he was determined to excel. The academy taught Schwarzkopf some valuable lessons, and he

At 6 feet 2 inches and 200 pounds, 16-year-old Norman Schwarzkopf played lineman on his high school football team at Valley Forge Military Academy. Schwarzkopf, the class valedictorian, graduated from Valley Forge in 1952.

remained grateful. Years later he wrote a letter to the school, saying, "West Point prepared me for the army. Valley Forge prepared me for life."

Despite a few minor disciplinary infractions, Schwarzkopf was an outstanding student at Valley Forge. In his senior year he was class valedictorian, a champion debater, a shot-putter on the track team, a football lineman, and editor of the class yearbook, *Crossed Sabres*. Although he was in charge of the yearbook, some of his classmates managed to insert a fictitious entry giving him the name Hugo, which he felt was much worse than Herbert would have been.

Schwarzkopf graduated from Valley Forge in 1952 at the head of a class of about 150 cadets. Life at the academy had confirmed his desire to enter West Point and the U.S. Army. One night he and fellow cadet Edward Hausberg were talking about their futures. Hausberg asked his friend what he wanted to do with his life.

"I want to be a general" was Schwarzkopf's reply. "I'll be very disappointed if I don't make general." Years later, Hausberg recalled that he "never doubted for an instant" that Schwarzkopf would reach his goal. "He did more in two years than most do in five or six," Hausberg said.

Schwarzkopf was awarded one of the coveted admissions to the U.S. Military Academy, and in the fall of 1952 he entered West Point for the four-year course that was to be both a college education and the foundation for a career as an army officer. West Point, a cluster of imposing stone buildings perched on a cliff overlooking the Hudson River north of New York City, was founded in 1802. Among its many traditions, none is more highly prized than honor. The Cadet chapel is decorated with plaques honoring the generals of the American Revolution, but the name on one plaque has been removed—it is the plaque of Benedict Arnold, the American officer who changed sides and was despised as a turncoat. As it so happened, West Point had endured an honor-code scandal in 1951, the year before Schwarzkopf enrolled, when some cadets on the football team had been caught violating the academy's strict honor code. As a result, greater emphasis than ever was placed on instilling honor, honesty, and integrity in the cadets of Schwarzkopf's class.

The Cadet chapel at the U.S. Military Academy in West Point, New York. Schwarzkopf entered the academy in the autumn of 1952.

Only three percent of the cadets who graduate from Valley Forge go on to have military careers, but West Point graduates are expected to serve in the U.S. Army for at least three years following graduation. For those who, like Norman Schwarzkopf, are hoping to make a life for themselves in the army's officer corps, West Point is an outstanding—although demanding—beginning.

One West Point tradition that was flourishing in 1952 was hazing, in which upperclassmen are allowed to give absurd or humiliating orders to first-year cadets, who are called plebes. Soon after Schwarzkopf entered the Point, the upperclassmen found out that his father had been the host of "Gangbusters," and from then on he had to imitate the show's opening sound effects—screaming sirens, screeching brakes, and rattling machine-gun fire—whenever he was ordered to do so by an older cadet. Schwarzkopf kept his temper during the hazing and even became rather good at the sound effects. He soon acquired the nickname "Schwarzie," the same nickname that his father had had during his own years at West Point.

A cadet's life at the Point revolves around three areas of activity: college classes, military training, and physical conditioning through sports. Schwarzkopf entered with gusto into all three. He performed well in classes and on exams, especially in the difficult courses in mechanical engineering, and at the end of 4 years he graduated in the top 10 percent of his class, ranking 42nd of 485 cadets. He did well in his military training, too, and became commander of his cadet company. His physical conditioning included football, wrestling, soccer, and tennis. Schwarzkopf took part in extracurricular activities as well. He improved his German in the German Club, and he pursued his love of music in the cadet choir, of which he was the leader during his senior year. And, like all cadets, he read widely in military history and engaged in long discussions with his classmates about leadership.

As a young man pursuing his studies in Europe, Schwarzkopf had read a great deal about history. He had particularly enjoyed reading about military campaigns and about the exploits of history's generals and military heroes: Alexander the Great, the Macedonian warrior-king who conquered nearly all of the known world in the 4th century B.C., and Hannibal, the Carthaginian general who brought troops and elephants across the Alps to defeat the

Schwarzkopf (indicated by the arrow) practices with the U.S. Military Academy's cadet choir in September 1955. During his senior year, Schwarzkopf became the leader of the choir.

mighty Roman army in 218 B.C. At West Point he studied military history more thoughtfully, trying to determine what it was that made a leader great. He identified what he thought was Alexander's most noteworthy quality: "Everything his troops did, he could do and better." He admired the fact that Alexander did not lead his men from afar but was himself part of every campaign.

That same quality of direct participation attracted him to two other military heroes, William T. Sherman and Ulysses S. Grant, who had been generals on the Union side during the American Civil War. Both were what he called "muddy boot soldiers" who respected their troops and, in turn, won respect and affection from those who served under them. Schwarzkopf said of Sherman that he "truly understood the horror of war but when required to execute a war, did so and hated every minute of it." Major General Leroy Suddath, who was Schwarzkopf's roommate at the Point, recalls that they used to read accounts of bygone battles and imagine what it would have been like to be in command on either side. Suddath adds that Schwarzkopf made no secret of his high ambitions. "Norm aimed for the top and expected to reach it," he says. Like many members of West Point's Class of 1956, Norman Schwarzkopf was determined to become a general. In all, 39 members of that class would reach the rank of general. Schwarzkopf was the first to become a four-star general.

Class standing is all-important at West Point, because cadets who graduate near the top of their class are assured a position in the branch of the U.S. Army they want to enter. They can select from among the artillery, engineering, armor, and other branches. A cadet like Schwarzkopf, with high class standing and an aptitude for mechanical engineering, is expected to join the artillery branch, which specializes in heavy guns and missiles. But Schwarzkopf had other ideas. He wanted to go into the infantry, the foot soldier's branch of the army.

The infantry is what most people think of when they think of soldiers. In combat, it is the infantrymen who actually engage with the enemy face-to-face. The infantry, although large and vitally important, is unglamorous. "There are many jokes about the different branches," says Lieutenant Colonel Robert D. Parrish in *Schwarzkopf: An Insider's View of the Commander and His Victory*, "but there is one thing everyone agrees on—the infantry is the toughest, most uncomfortable, most dangerous and, some would say, most unappreciated branch in the Army." But it is also the most important branch of the army, the one that all the other branches are designed to support, and this appealed to Schwarzkopf.

During his senior year, he and some of his fellow cadets led an effort at West Point to rouse enthusiasm for the

William Tecumseh Sherman (1820–91) served as a Union general during the American Civil War (1861–65). Schwarzkopf admired Sherman because he was a "muddy boot soldier" who respected his troops.

infantry. By night they nailed models of the combat infantryman's badge to trees on campus. This underground movement was so successful that a high percentage of graduating cadets in 1956 chose the infantry as their branch of the army. Schwarzkopf was among them, and his choice did not entirely please his father, who retired from the army that same year. The senior Schwarzkopf had expected his son to choose a more sophisticated, technological branch, such as artillery. Schwarzkopf says of his father's reaction, "I think he thought I was never going to go anywhere; he was convinced the high-tech Army was the place to be. If my dad were alive today he'd be amazed that, as a mud-foot infantryman, I've gone from second lieutenant all the way to four-star general." Herbert Norman Schwarzkopf died in 1958, two years after Schwarzkopf, Jr., graduated from West Point. The father had seen the son launched on his long-dreamed-of army career, but he did not live long enough to see how high that career would rise.

Upon his graduation from West Point, Schwarzkopf was commissioned as a second lieutenant in the army. This, the lowest rank among commissioned officers, is where everyone starts; from then on, an officer's progress is measured, in part, by how rapidly he or she moves up

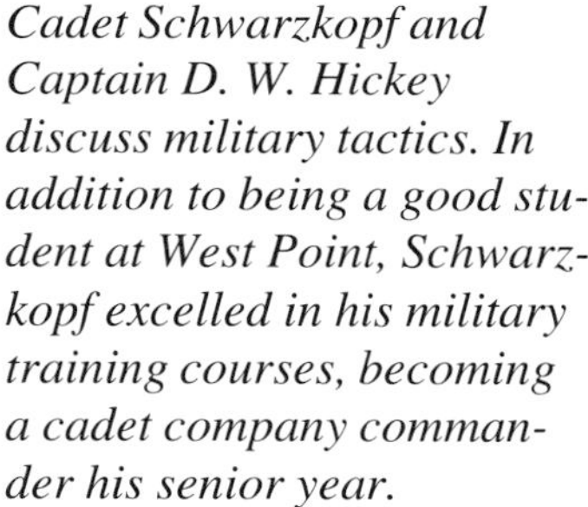

Cadet Schwarzkopf and Captain D. W. Hickey discuss military tactics. In addition to being a good student at West Point, Schwarzkopf excelled in his military training courses, becoming a cadet company commander his senior year.

Recruits learn to parachute at the army's infantry school at Fort Benning, Georgia. After graduating from West Point, Second Lieutenant Schwarzkopf entered a six-month basic training course in which he earned his paratrooper badge.

through the ranks. Schwarzkopf reported to Fort Benning, Georgia, for the six-month Basic Infantry Course, the first phase of the army's system of professional education for its officers. Courses beyond the basic course are selective, which means that an officer has to be chosen by his or her superiors to attend them. Being selected for an elite course is a sign that an officer is well regarded and that his or her career is on the rise. For the next decade or so, Schwarzkopf, like every other young officer, would anxiously scan each new school list, hoping to see his own name and the names of his friends.

The Basic Infantry Course included paratrooper training. Schwarzkopf learned to parachute, fully armed and combat ready, from an airplane, and by the end of the course he was entitled to wear the badge of a paratrooper, a pair of tiny silver wings. Then he reported to his first duty posting, at Fort Campbell, Kentucky. Schwarzkopf was responsible for training enlisted soldiers and also for carrying out numerous dull tasks that were handed over to the lowest-ranking officer, such as inspecting the mess hall or inventorying the stock of the officers' club.

Schwarzkopf fulfilled his responsibilities well and was promoted to first lieutenant. During his two years at Fort Campbell, however, he came to the first of several crossroads in his army career. He grew disgusted with the failings and inefficiency of the people around him and considered leaving the army. As he explains, "I had an alcoholic commander and an executive officer who was a coward. I saw terrible things going on around me and I said, 'Who needs it? When my three years are up, I'm getting out!'"

At that point, Schwarzkopf says, someone sat him down and told him, "Young man, you know, if all the guys who see these bad things happening quit, then all the guys who don't think these things are so bad are going to be doing them later on. If you really think it's that bad, why don't you stick around until someday you get into a position to do something about it?" Schwarzkopf thought it over and decided to follow this advice. He still believed that the army was, or should be, a fine and honorable institution. He resolved not to let a bad experience with one posting drive him away from what had been his lifelong dream—to serve in his country's armed forces.

In July 1959, Schwarzkopf received a new posting. In another parallel with his father's career, he was sent to Berlin, one of the most desirable postings in the army, with sophisticated nightlife, a chance to travel around Europe, and excellent training opportunities for young officers. The cold war tension between the non-Communist Western powers and the Soviet sponsors of East Germany was increasing, and Berlin was the center of much political activity. From an army officer's point of view, the Berlin Brigade was one of the few outfits in which a commander could conduct maneuvers with tanks and armored personnel carriers just about anywhere in the area.

As a platoon leader in Berlin, Schwarzkopf was responsible for the performance of the men in his unit during sudden alerts—unannounced drills that often took place in

the middle of the night. Each unit had to rush to its combat position, with all gear in full operational readiness. If a truck failed to start or a soldier's equipment was not in proper shape, Lieutenant Schwarzkopf would suffer for it. So he kept his men on their toes and began to develop a reputation as a no-nonsense commanding officer.

Using binoculars, U.S. soldiers peer over the Berlin Wall in 1964. Schwarzkopf's two-year tour in Berlin ended in 1961, just as the East German government began to erect the wall that sealed off West Berlin from East Berlin and East Germany.

During Schwarzkopf's second year in Berlin, he served as aide-de-camp, or assistant, to the U.S. Army's commanding general in Berlin. The officers chosen to be aides-de-camp are those who are thought to show considerable promise, because the job offers a chance to see how top-level officers operate. Although an aide-de-camp's position is in some ways privileged, it is also difficult, requiring tact and diplomacy. A young officer who fails to demonstrate these qualities during a term as aide-de-camp to a commander is unlikely to advance very far. The signs of Schwarzkopf's progress, however, were clear.

In July 1961, just as the Berlin Wall was being erected by the East German government to divide West Berlin from East Berlin, Schwarzkopf was promoted to the rank of captain and sent back to Fort Benning, Georgia, for the yearlong Infantry Officers' Advanced Course. By the time he graduated from the course, he was qualified to wear a master parachutist's badge. He had also begun to experience chronic back pain—caused in large part by his parachute jumps—that would trouble him for a decade.

The army now gave Captain Schwarzkopf a clear signal that it was pleased with his progress and had marked him for further advancement. It sent him to the University of Southern California (USC) in Los Angeles to earn his

An aerial view of the U.S. Military Academy. After earning a master's degree in mechanical and aerospace engineering, Schwarzkopf returned to West Point and taught mechanical engineering during the 1964–65 academic year.

master's degree. A full course of study at a civilian university is expensive, and only a select few career officers receive these prize assignments. Schwarzkopf enrolled in USC in 1962 and spent two years in the California sunshine, studying missile mechanics and aerospace engineering.

It was a good time for an army officer to master this subject. A few years earlier, in 1957, the United States had been shocked and alarmed when the Soviet Union sent several *Sputnik* satellites into space. America's educational, technological, and military communities felt the pressure to catch up with the Soviets—fast. The United States launched its first space vehicles in 1958, and by 1964, when Schwarzkopf graduated from USC with his master's degree in mechanical and aerospace engineering, the nation's space program was under way. That July, the U.S. *Ranger 7* probe reached the moon.

The army had invested in Schwarzkopf's advanced training, and he was expected to repay that investment by sharing his technical knowledge. He was assigned to teach mechanical engineering at West Point for three years. In the fall of 1964, 12 years after coming to the Point as a plebe, he returned as an instructor.

Schwarzkopf loved the Point, but he was dissatisfied there during the 1964–65 academic year. There was a war going on in Asia, and the man who had chosen the "mud soldier's" branch of the service did not want to sit out the war in a classroom. He volunteered for active duty and was told that he could be sent overseas to the combat zone if he agreed to complete his teaching obligation afterward. He agreed, and in June 1965 he was put on a Military Air Command flight to Vietnam, a small country in Southeast Asia.

At the time, most Americans could not even locate Vietnam on a map. Before long, however, the conflict that was raging under the jungle canopy of this obscure land would occupy the center of the world stage.

On August 7, 1965, Major Schwarzkopf (left) helps carry a South Vietnamese paratrooper wounded during a North Vietnamese mortar attack on an outpost at Duc Co. Schwarzkopf served two tours of duty in Vietnam, 1965–66 and 1969–70.

4

Silver Stars and Friendly Fire

VIETNAM WAS A DIVIDED COUNTRY that American military strategists believed was vital to U.S. interests. A strip of fertile, mountainous land along the eastern side of the peninsula of Southeast Asia, it was occupied by a people who were ethnically related to both the people of Thailand and those of China. In the 19th century, France seized control of Vietnam and governed it as a colony. After many uprisings against colonial rule, the Vietnamese finally drove the French out in 1954. At that time, various factions among the Vietnamese were vying for control. The rival groups signed a treaty that divided Vietnam into two countries, North Vietnam and South Vietnam.

North Vietnam, with its capital in Hanoi, had a Communist government, sponsored by the Communist regimes of the People's Republic of China and the Soviet Union. South Vietnam, with its capital in Saigon, was a nominal republic backed by the United States, which interfered in local politics to put power into the hands of officials who favored close ties with the United States. When the country was divided in 1954, it was planned that the two Vietnams would be reunited in 1956 under a government chosen by the people. But the South Vietnamese regime, with the support of the United States, refused to hold reunification elections because it was convinced that the government of North Vietnam, headed by Ho Chi Minh, would prevail. North and South Vietnam were to remain separate and at war with one another for more than 20 years.

In December 1960, the North Vietnamese government formed the National Liberation Front (NLF), a Communist-led alliance of various religious, nationalist, and socialist groups. NLF guerrillas—called the Vietcong by the South Vietnamese—began launching raids on the Saigon government. State officials, teachers, and health workers were kidnapped or assassinated; roads and communication lines were destroyed; and military outposts were attacked.

South Vietnam, in the meanwhile, was receiving money, weapons, and other forms of aid from the United States, which did not want Communist North Vietnam to gain control of the entire country. The late 1950s and the 1960s were a time of extreme hostility between the Communist and the non-Communist superpowers, each of whom sought to build up support among the smaller nations of the world. Strategists in the United States feared that if South Vietnam fell to the Communists, the other nations of Southeast Asia would follow like a row of collapsing dominoes. So in order to prevent the Communist takeover of Southeast Asia, the United States vowed to support the South Vietnamese government.

In the early 1960s, U.S. support took the form of advisers, military officers, and other experts who helped the South Vietnamese organize and train their troops and develop battle plans. After becoming president in November 1963 upon the death of President John F. Kennedy, Lyndon B. Johnson tried to calm the fears of Americans who thought that the United States was about to become

A U.S. Army adviser (second from left) chats with a South Vietnamese officer in May 1966. The United States began providing military advisers to the South Vietnamese government in 1962. More than 15,000 U.S. military advisers were stationed in Vietnam by December 1963.

seriously embroiled in an Asian war. "We are not about to send American boys nine or ten thousand miles from home to do what Asian boys ought to be doing for themselves," he said. But by the time Norman Schwarzkopf arrived in Saigon in June 1965, there were about 80,000 Americans in Vietnam, and more were on the way. They were coming not just to advise but to fight. A massive buildup was beginning; by January 1969 the U.S. troop count in Vietnam would reach a high of 534,000.

In the summer of 1965, however, many American officers were still serving as advisers to the Vietnamese. There were two kinds of advisers—staff advisers and field advisers. Staff advisers worked with high-ranking Vietnamese staff officers at headquarters bases but did not go out into the bush, where the fighting took place. Field advisers, on the other hand, lived with their Vietnamese units and went into combat with them. Schwarzkopf, promoted to the rank of major upon his arrival in Vietnam, was made a field adviser. The field advisers were supposed to try to blend in with their Vietnamese counterparts so that they would not be singled out for attack in firefights with the Vietcong. Schwarzkopf therefore adopted the uniform of the Vietnamese airborne unit to which he was assigned, but his towering height and 240-pound frame ruined his attempt to blend in with the much smaller Vietnamese.

Schwarzkopf's unit was stationed in the central highlands of Vietnam, an area where both the North Vietnamese army and the Vietcong had been especially active. By 1965, the Communist forces had nearly taken complete control of the countryside. Both the South Vietnamese army and the anti-Communist guerrilla fighters of the Montagnards, as the local mountain-dwelling people were called, were struggling to hold the Vietcong at bay. Schwarzkopf and his men had to be constantly alert in case of an ambush or a sudden attack.

Schwarzkopf saw plenty of action during his tour of duty. Around the time he reached Vietnam, a force of 3,000 North Vietnamese attacked Duc Co, an outpost manned by 400 South Vietnamese and a dozen American advisers. The defenders of Duc Co held off the assault, but they were

U.S. Army infantrymen take aim at Vietcong guerrillas during a firefight near Quang Ngai. The first U.S. combat troops arrived in Vietnam in March 1965; by the end of 1966, U.S. troops numbered nearly 400,000.

surrounded. For several months, they survived on food and ammunition that were dropped into their camp every day by supply planes. Then the attack intensified, and Duc Co was in danger of being overrun. A thousand South Vietnamese airborne troops parachuted into the camp to break the siege. They were accompanied by a handful of advisers, including Schwarzkopf, newly arrived in Vietnam. Despite heavy bombardment from the artillery in the camp and from the South Vietnamese air forces, the North Vietnamese refused to pull back from Duc Co. Groups of South Vietnamese, including Schwarzkopf's unit, went into the jungle to try to drive the enemy back. Schwarzkopf's unit got split up, and the major made his way through enemy fire to get several wounded paratroopers back into the relative safety of the camp. He then went out once more into the firefight to locate and reunite the scattered groups of his unit. It was not until late August that the siege of Duc Co was broken, by a U.S. airborne brigade. Schwarzkopf was awarded a Silver Star for the bravery that he had shown in rescuing the injured men and reorganizing the unit.

South Vietnamese paratroopers conduct a practice jump. Schwarzkopf served as a field adviser to a South Vietnames airborne unit during his first tour of duty in Vietnam.

He won a second Silver Star in February 1966 for leading a parachute assault on a Vietcong position. In order to get a good view of the action so that he could tell his men where to fire, he exposed himself to enemy attack and received four wounds, although he refused medical evacuation until all the wounded Vietnamese had been airlifted out. Schwarzkopf was also awarded a Bronze Star during this tour of duty for unloading a helicopter in the midst of enemy fire and getting wounded soldiers safely into it and off the battlefield.

Schwarzkopf's tour of duty as an adviser was not all heroism and awards, however. It also introduced him to some elements of war that he found absurd. As a result, he had several explosive outbursts of temper. One incident occurred soon after his arrival in Vietnam. He advised the South Vietnamese officers of his airborne unit not to go

Army medics carry wounded U.S. soldiers from a Huey helicopter to a field hospital. In 1966, Schwarzkopf received a Bronze Star for loading wounded soldiers onto a helicopter in the midst of enemy fire.

into a battle during a campaign in the Ia Drang Valley. He was promptly called up before a board of senior Vietnamese officers who had planned the battle. They demanded to know why he had dared to give advice that went against their orders. He told them bluntly that in his opinion they had not ordered enough artillery and aircraft support to protect the paratroopers. "Of course they were furious," he says. "But that's my approach to military operations. You're talking human lives, and my responsibility is to accomplish the objective with the minimum loss of the troops under my command. That's my job—not just accomplishing the mission." Schwarzkopf was not afraid to tangle with the top brass, as high-ranking officers are called, if he felt that soldiers' lives were being needlessly risked.

A second outburst of temper occurred during the siege of Duc Co. After 10 long days of defensive fighting, his unit had sustained serious casualties. Some of his Vietnamese paratroopers were wounded, lying on the ground and waiting to be evacuated. Schwarzkopf got on the radio and called all over the area, trying to find a helicopter to pick them up. He was infuriated to discover that all the helicopters were tied up on special trips for VIPs—Very Important Persons, such as high-level officers, South Vietnamese government officials, or visiting congressional delegates. "I can still remember it to this day," Schwarzkopf told an interviewer years later, "because I was yelling profanities over the airwaves."

That incident, Schwarzkopf says, began the reputation of his well-known temper, which occasionally blasts forth to scorch anyone in the vicinity—although his associates point out that it dies down as quickly as it explodes and that Schwarzkopf never holds a grudge. After that first tour in Vietnam, he explains, "I can remember subsequently getting back to the States and suddenly I would lose my temper. How shocked I was; it had never happened before." He adds, "I do not get mad at people; I get mad at things that happen; I get mad at betrayal of trust; I get angry at lack of consideration for the soldiers. And contrary to what's been said, I do not throw things. If somebody happens to be in my burst radius when I go off, I make very sure they understand it's not them I'm angry at. Having said that, any time a guy who's six-foot-three and weighs 240 pounds and wears four stars loses his temper, everybody runs for cover. I recognize that, but I don't think I'm abusive. There's a difference."

Schwarzkopf had another disillusionment at Duc Co. When the siege was finally lifted, a flock of helicopters descended, bearing General William Westmoreland, commander of U.S. forces in Vietnam, and dozens of news reporters and dignitaries. Westmoreland asked for the senior American adviser, and Schwarzkopf stepped forward and identified himself. Westmoreland then excused himself from the reporters and asked for a moment alone with Schwarzkopf. The two walked off a few paces. Schwarzkopf was keyed up with excitement, expecting a soldierly insight or a private word of encouragement from his commanding officer. But all that Westmoreland said was "Major, how's the food?" Schwarzkopf explained that because of the siege the troops had been living on rations from the air drops. Westmoreland was silent for a minute and then asked, "Well, Major, are you getting your mail?"

Much later, Schwarzkopf admitted that he had quite a low opinion of Westmoreland, who sometimes seemed more concerned with the media and the politicians than with the men under his command. He had great respect and admiration, however, for General Creighton Abrams, who in 1968 replaced Westmoreland as commander of U.S. forces in Vietnam. Abrams represented for Schwarzkopf "what the professional military should be all about. He was totally candid. He had a great expression that I used to think about a lot. He said, 'Did you ever think what a great army it would be if no one worried about who got the credit?' That's the way I like to do things," says Schwarzkopf. "Get the job done and then sort out the credit later."

After a little more than a year in Vietnam, Major Schwarzkopf was assigned back to West Point to resume his teaching responsibilities. Schwarzkopf now says that despite the discomforts and dangers that he had faced in the war zone of an unfamiliar land, his first tour of duty in Vietnam was the best year of his life. Often he slept on the ground and had to make do with grim survival rations, but he was happy to be doing the job for which he had been trained in the service of his country. "After my first tour I came home with probably the greatest feeling of satisfaction I've ever had in anything I've ever done," he said in 1971. Although there were those back home who opposed U.S. involvement in Vietnamese affairs, for Schwarzkopf the situation was simple: He was a soldier. It was not his job to make policy or to criticize those who did so. If his superior officers, acting on the orders of the president, told him to fight on behalf of a U.S. ally, then it was his business to fight. "It was truly serving a cause I believed in," he recalls. He later told author C. D. B. Bryan, "We fought almost every day of every month for thirteen months. I really thought we had done something good, like George Washington. I had gone and fought for freedom."

He found that not everyone cared. When he arrived at the airport in New York City on his way home, no one paid any attention to his uniform. He took a cab to his mother's house, expecting the cab driver to ask if he was just back from Vietnam. The driver said nothing, even when Schwarzkopf remarked, "Sure is great to be back in the U.S. again!" It was then that he began to realize that the veterans of Vietnam were not going to be regarded as heroes at home.

His sister Sally saw a difference in her brother upon his return from Vietnam. "After the first tour, he lost his youth when he came back—this light, wonderful youth that young men have," she says. "He recovered it, but when he first came back he was very serious. It made a deep impression on me." Everyone who fought in Vietnam was marked by the experience, and for Schwarzkopf, the deeper scars were yet to come.

He spent the next two years as an instructor at West Point. It was an eventful time for him because, at the age of 33, after dating many women but becoming seriously involved with none of them, he fell in love. In 1967 a vivacious, brown-haired, 26-year-old flight attendant named Brenda Holsinger attended a football game at West Point. She met some friends there, and they told her about a man they would like to introduce her to that night at the officers' club. She went with them to the club, and when a tall, rugged-looking major walked in, she said to herself, "Gee, it would be nice if that's who they're going to introduce me to." It so happened that the tall major, Norman Schwarzkopf, was the very fellow her friends had in mind. The two were introduced and started dating the next week. Two weeks later they were engaged.

General William Westmoreland, commander of U.S. combat forces in Vietnam, greets soldiers arriving in South Vietnam in September 1965. Schwarzkopf became dissatisfied with Westmoreland because he felt that the general was more concerned about politics and media relations than about his troops.

On July 6, 1968, newlyweds Norman and Brenda Schwarzkopf emerge from the chapel at West Point. They prepare to pass under the crossed sabers—a tradition at weddings of military officers.

They were married on July 6, 1968, in the chapel at West Point. By then Schwarzkopf had completed his three years of teaching. After a honeymoon in Jamaica, he and his new wife set out for Fort Leavenworth, Kansas. Schwarzkopf had been selected to attend the army's Command and General Staff College there. Only about 35 percent of the eligible officers are chosen for this yearlong course, which trains officers in the wartime and peacetime operations of large units such as divisions, corps, and armies. It also prepares them for appointments in the Department of Defense, the North Atlantic Treaty Organization (NATO), or other high-level staff positions. At the same time, Schwarzkopf was promoted to the rank of lieutenant colonel, about a year ahead of most majors his age.

A year at Fort Leavenworth was a good introduction to army life for Brenda Schwarzkopf, who was nervous about fitting in. Before their marriage, Schwarzkopf had explained to her that being a military wife could be stressful. She would have to be prepared to move anywhere at any time, whenever the army changed his posting, regardless of whether they had children in school or friends in the community. He also warned her that if the army sent him on a special mission he might simply say to her, "I have to leave. I can't tell you where I'm going or how long I'll be gone." These prospects did not scare Brenda away, but she knew that the world of army officers—and their spouses—had its own customs, traditions, and even language, all of which she would have to learn.

"In our first assignment," she recalls, "we were going to be with soldiers and a brigade and a company and a battalion. I knew nothing about any of this. So I had an awful lot to learn and I was a little bit scared about it the first time we went to that assignment. My husband's words were to me then as they are still today, 'Brenda, just be yourself and it will all work out.'" It did work out, and Brenda Schwarzkopf adapted to the particular trials that an army officer's spouse must face. Among other things, she moved 16 times in 20 years as her husband's postings took them around the country and the world.

When Schwarzkopf's time at Fort Leavenworth was over, he told Brenda that he wanted to volunteer for a second tour of duty in Vietnam. He felt that he had a responsibility to be where the fighting was. She did not try to change his mind. Instead, she settled into the Washington, D.C., area and continued to work as a flight attendant. And in July 1969, less than a year after his wedding, Lieutenant Colonel Schwarzkopf returned to Vietnam.

Much had changed in the three years that Schwarzkopf had been away from Vietnam. American troop strength had passed the half-million mark. Casualties were high. U.S. aircraft had made hundreds of bombing runs over the neighboring countries of Cambodia and Laos, destroying not only the hidden bases of the Communists and their sympathizers but also scores of civilian villages. Yet North Vietnam continued to send supplies and infiltrators into South Vietnam. Many American officers and soldiers believed that if the United States went all out to win the war, it could easily subdue North Vietnam. But an all-out, no-holds-barred attack was never authorized. It seemed to many that the United States had gotten far enough into the war to suffer tremendous losses, but not far enough to win it.

Army officers in Vietnam resented that the government policymakers back in Washington could not seem to make up their minds about what they really wanted to do in Vietnam. But this indecision reflected the fact that the United States itself was deeply divided over what was happening in Southeast Asia. Many citizens and members of Congress felt that the United States had a responsibility to prosecute the war and could not abandon South Vietnam to the Communists. But a growing number of Americans disagreed; they claimed that the United States had no business fighting what was essentially another country's civil war and should not be mounting air attacks on Vietnam's neutral neighbors.

Antiwar sentiment had been strong in the United States since 1967. Thousands of protesters, many of them college

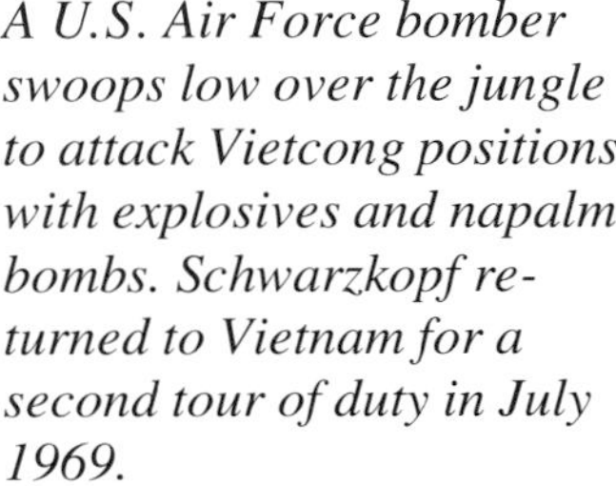

A U.S. Air Force bomber swoops low over the jungle to attack Vietcong positions with explosives and napalm bombs. Schwarzkopf returned to Vietnam for a second tour of duty in July 1969.

students, marched on the Pentagon and down the streets of New York City, calling for an end to the war. Public opinion polls showed that a substantial percentage of Americans—a majority, according to some polls—disapproved of U.S. involvement in the war. President Richard M. Nixon, responding to the growing pressure from the public to get the United States out of Vietnam, had announced a policy of Vietnamization that was supposed to turn the war back over to South Vietnamese nationals. American troops, he said, would gradually be withdrawn. In June 1969, the same month that Schwarzkopf went back to Vietnam, Nixon announced that 25,000 American soldiers would return home.

But the war was far from over, as Schwarzkopf was to discover. He was appalled by the condition of the army he found upon his return to Vietnam: "It was a cesspool," he said. The morale of both officers and enlisted men was low. Poorly prepared for jungle warfare, many men became weak and ill. Heroin and other drugs were readily available and had become a serious problem among the soldiers. Disciplinary incidents were on the rise, and some officers seemed more concerned about having a good time at parties in Saigon than about the welfare of the grunts, the foot soldiers in the bush. Junior officers in the field, many of them young and inexperienced, had to cope with another problem as well: the senior officers who cruised over combat areas in helicopters, looking for action. When they spotted a hot spot—a firefight or other activity—they would hover at a safe distance and radio down instructions to the team on the ground. Schwarzkopf reports that sometimes four or five helicopters filled with top brass would circle over a hot spot while, down below, a beleaguered lieutenant or captain and his grunts grappled with the Vietcong.

Because of the growing unpopularity of the war at home, the army was pressured to produce high body counts—that is, estimates of the number of enemy dead and wounded—that might justify the U.S. presence in Vietnam and quiet the criticism that was being leveled against the war effort. Like every other officer in Vietnam, Schwarzkopf saw that body counts were often inflated or simply falsified to please the higher-ups. He also saw that poorly trained and managed U.S. troops were sustaining higher casualties than he believed were necessary, sometimes while failing to inflict many casualties on the enemy. Cynicism and brutality seemed to be eroding the values of duty, honor, and patriotism that he thought were supposed to be at the heart of military service. His first year in Vietnam had been the best year of his life; his second year there was the worst.

He spent the first five months of it behind a desk in staff headquarters at an air base outside Saigon. Then he got what he really wanted, command of a field battalion. He was assigned to the Americal Division, which was fighting in the coastal plains. It was here that the rescue of the wounded soldier from the Batangan minefield, which earned Schwarzkopf his third Silver Star, took place. But in February 1970, a few months before the minefield rescue, an incident occurred in his battalion that was to have far-reaching consequences.

Two soldiers under Schwarzkopf's command were killed when a shell fired from an American artillery gun—part of a barrage that was supposed to defend the soldiers' own position—struck a tree and exploded right above them. When a soldier is killed by a bullet or missile fired from his own side, the death is said to have been caused by "friendly fire." Such casualties are inevitable, especially in a large-scale conflict, and they are generally the result of chance rather than negligence or incompetence. But the parents of Michael Mullen, one of the dead soldiers, were distressed to learn that their son had died as a result of friendly fire. They grew angry when the army refused to respond to their requests for more information, and they

In 1967, a peace demonstrator taunts military police in front of the Pentagon. By the time Schwarzkopf returned to Vietnam in 1969 for his second tour of duty, sentiment against involvement in the Vietnam War had grown strong in the United States.

focused their anger on Schwarzkopf, blaming him for their son's death and accusing him of covering up the facts afterward. Back home in Iowa, they became antiwar activists, stirring up feeling against the war. Schwarzkopf was one of their targets.

Author C. D. B. Bryan became interested in the Mullens' story and interviewed them at length. Then he interviewed Schwarzkopf. He published the results of his investigation in a best-selling book called *Friendly Fire* (1976), which was made into a television movie. Bryan came to the conclusion that Schwarzkopf was not responsible for Michael Mullen's death—in fact, he had been with another unit in the battalion, at a different location, on the night Mullen was killed. Mullen's death, Bryan decided, was just what Schwarzkopf said it was: a tragic accident.

Bryan further concluded that, although the Pentagon's handling of the Mullens' inquiries had been insensitive and even devious, Schwarzkopf was not involved in any cover-up. He felt that Schwarzkopf was an honest and compassionate commanding officer. This opinion was shared by many of Schwarzkopf's men and fellow officers, as well as by many civilians who knew him. The Mullens, however, continued to regard Schwarzkopf as a bloodthirsty officer who callously sacrificed his men to advance his own career.

An infantryman who served under Schwarzkopf, Martin Culpepper, shared the Mullens' view. Culpepper is quoted in Jack Anderson and Dale van Atta's book *Stormin' Norman: An American Hero* (1991) as saying, "He didn't care about us. I was just a piece of meat without any consideration. As for his character, he was known as 'Buddy Butcher.' I never heard anyone call him 'Stormin' Norman' or 'the Bear.'" The Vietnam experience was destructive or demoralizing for nearly every soldier there, and a fair number of them blamed or resented their commanding officers, not always unjustly. Like every other commander in Vietnam, Schwarzkopf left behind a legacy laced with bitterness. He is confident, however, that he always did his best for the men under his command. He says that his "first and foremost reason" for returning to Vietnam for his second tour of duty was that "based upon my experience, that first tour with the Vietnamese Airborne, I felt I definitely had something I could contribute as a battalion commander. I felt I could accomplish the mission with the minimum loss of life—none, if possible, which is what it's all about, really."

In July 1970, six weeks after the episode in the minefield of Batangan, Schwarzkopf's tour of duty ended. For the second time he flew home from Vietnam. The lack of excitement that he had encountered on his first return had disappointed him, but the hostility that he met this time infuriated him. Antiwar feeling had risen to a fever pitch.

Some antiwar activists spat on the uniforms of returning soldiers and taunted them with cries of "murderer!" and "baby-killer!" Schwarzkopf gave speeches to civic clubs, and people in the audience stood up and accused him of bombing villages and murdering babies. Such treatment stung him personally, because he knew he was guilty of no such atrocities, but it also hurt him that the army had fallen into such widespread, general disrespect. Even people who felt sympathetic toward the returning soldiers were often afraid to show their sympathy, because in some circles it was regarded as unfashionably militaristic.

Schwarzkopf told author Bryan that for many veterans, coming home from Vietnam was like having surgery for cancer: "When it's all over you've got the scar, number one; and number two, you're not really ever sure that you got it all out of your system. You never know when it's going to rear its ugly head again. But if you're going to live your life, you're going to have to learn to live with that."

It took several years for Schwarzkopf to come to terms with his own Vietnam experience. At first he was able to swallow his misgivings about the war and the army in the joy of his reunion with Brenda; they had seen each other only once during his second tour of duty, when they met in Hong Kong for a week. They settled into a home in Annandale, Virginia, and Schwarzkopf took up a staff job at Fort McNair, near Washington, D.C. Their first child, a girl, was born the month after Schwarzkopf's return. They named her Cynthia. A second daughter, Jessica, was born in 1972.

In 1971, Schwarzkopf enered Walter Reed Army Medical Center. The back pain he had endured ever since he started playing football in high school and college had grown worse during his paratrooper training, and now it was unbearable. X rays showed that his spine was fractured; surgery was needed to correct it. He spent months encased in a body cast while his back healed. In the hospital he was visited by the suspicious and resentful Mullens,

Schwarzkopf enjoys breakfast at his Virginia home with his niece and nephew.

who were trying to investigate their son's death, and soon afterward he was interviewed by Bryan, who was researching *Friendly Fire*. Another reminder of Vietnam was Robert Trabbert, the artillery officer who had been so horribly wounded in the Batangan minefield explosion. Trabbert was being treated in Walter Reed while Schwarzkopf was there.

Recalling episodes from his own Vietnam experience, and witnessing the contempt that many people showed for the army and its soldiers, Schwarzkopf occasionally came close to despair. He thought about leaving the army. He told himself that he was skilled enough and young enough to get a good job and start life over as a civilian. "There were times," he said later to Bryan, "when I was tempted to just bail out and go build myself a cabin in the wilderness and commune with nature."

Schwarzkopf's emotional healing began in the spring of 1972, around the time his second daughter, Jessica, was born. He and Brenda were still living in Annandale. His sister Sally came over one night to watch a movie on television, and the three sat in the living room drinking wine. The movie was a war picture, and in one scene a group of men started crossing a minefield. "You just knew any damn minute some damn mine was going to go off," Schwarzkopf recalls, "something you had been through a thousand times in real life, and all of a sudden the mine went off and people were blowing up."

Schwarzkopf broke into a sweat and began trembling, and when Sally asked him what was the matter, he tried to explain his emotions: what Vietnam had been like and how it hurt not to be appreciated at home. Sally was opposed to the war. She suggested that maybe the antiwar protesters were right. Schwarzkopf was so upset to hear these words from his beloved sister that he began to cry, and he ordered Sally, who was also crying, to leave the house. When he woke up the next morning, he realized that he had been wrong. He could not deny anyone—especially someone he knew and trusted—the right to an independent opinion. He and Sally apologized to one another, and their closeness was restored. But Schwarzkopf realized that morning that Vietnam had raised some powerful, volatile emotions in him.

"I recognized that . . . whatever it was eating me away could absolutely destroy me if I didn't get a handle on it," he told C. D. B. Bryan later. And he told a Seattle reporter in 1986, "I thought a lot about the role of the army and my place in it after the Vietnam War, as I think any professional who had any sensitivity at all had to do." Finally, he came to the same conclusion he had reached years earlier, when he first considered leaving the army. He decided that if he were ever given an order that would make him violate his moral principles, he would stick by his principles and resign from the army. But until that happened, he would stay in the army as long as he felt he could help improve it. With all its faults, it was still the life he loved.

Schwarzkopf posed for this portrait when he was promoted to the rank of lieutenant colonel in 1974. Four years later, he was promoted to the rank of brigadier general.

5

War in the Caribbean

AFTER SEVERAL YEARS as a member of the U.S. Army's personnel staff in Washington, D.C., Schwarzkopf was selected to attend one of the service's most prestigious schools, the Army War College in Carlisle, Pennsylvania. During his year in Carlisle, he took part in seminars and discussion groups that ranged across many aspects of national and international affairs. Everyone knew that the officers who attended the War College were the pool from which future generals would be chosen, and now that he felt himself getting close, Norman Schwarzkopf was more determined than ever to be one of those generals.

His next posting took him back to Washington for a staff job at the Pentagon in the financial management office of the army. The Pentagon is the headquarters of the Department of Defense, which is the administrative institution responsible for the activities of the U.S. Army, Navy, Air Force, and Marine Corps. Although career officers are expected to put in stints of Pentagon duty, Schwarzkopf hated desk jobs and yearned to have soldiers under his command. So when he was offered a chance to become deputy commander of Fort Richardson, near Anchorage, Alaska, he accepted eagerly—in spite of Alaska's bitterly cold winters and mosquito-infested summers. He was so glad to be a field officer again that he threw his troops into a grueling round of training exercises, including an 11-day simulated battle that involved 4,000 soldiers. He worked hard and demanded hard work from everyone in his command. He was promoted to the rank of full colonel in 1975.

The same year that Schwarzkopf made colonel, his mother died. In the months and years that followed, although his duties as a military commander demanded much of his schedule, he found time to share many activities with his own children. He believed in the importance of close family ties and encouraged family-oriented social events at his postings.

Fort Richardson had an impressive setting, overlooked by the glaciers of the Chugach mountain range and by the towering peak of Mount Denali (formerly called Mount McKinley), North America's highest mountain. Schwarzkopf fell in love with the vast Alaskan wilderness and became convinced of the need to preserve and protect the natural environment. He, Brenda, and the girls took trips into the countryside with a camping trailer. Schwarzkopf

In 1975, Lt. Colonel Schwarzkopf—deputy commander of Fort Richardson, near Anchorage, Alaska—leads the 172nd Infantry Brigade on a 68-mile march. He gained a reputation for leading his troops through rigorous training exercises.

also loved to take long hiking and fishing trips, sometimes alone. Once he persuaded Sally to visit for two weeks and flew her to a remote river for some salmon fishing.

Schwarzkopf's passion for the outdoors was kept alive by his next assignment, which was at Fort Lewis, near Tacoma in Washington State. For the first time, he was in full command of a brigade (3,000 infantry soldiers). He drilled them relentlessly, but his commanding general noted, "He was a real maker of military leaders. He wasn't interested in climbing ranks. He was interested in his men." Occasionally, however, Schwarzkopf managed hiking or hunting excursions into the Washington mountains. One fellow officer remembers a long day of bird hunting in the Yakima Valley. Not only had they not shot any birds, they had not even *seen* any. But after they toiled up a steep ridge on the way home, Schwarzkopf stood looking at the magnificent sunset view and happily boomed out, "Great day to be alive in the Yakima!" On rainy days, when the steady downpour turned the parade ground into ankle-deep mud that clung to the soldiers' boots, Schwarzkopf would stand reviewing his troops and bellow, "Great day to be a soldier!"

The Schwarzkopfs spent the years 1976–78 at Fort Lewis. Their third child, a son whom they named Christian, after Schwarzkopf's grandfather, was born there in 1977. Then, in the spring of 1978, Schwarzkopf and several dozen other outstanding colonels were called to Washington, D.C., for a six-week course that the army calls "charm school." It is an orientation designed to prepare colonels for promotion to the rank of general. Schwarzkopf got his long-anticipated promotion to brigadier general, the first rank of general, in August. Brenda helped him pin his first general's star onto his uniform collar, and then he took up a new posting in Hawaii, where he served as a staff officer in the Department of Defense's Pacific Command. This is a joint, or combined, command center for the U.S. Army, Navy, and

Air Force, with representatives from all forces. Schwarzkopf's comfortable desk job gave him the chance to take up scuba diving and explore the tropical paradise of Hawaii, but he was still restless. He had no soldiers in his command.

He was glad when his tour in Hawaii ended and he returned to field command. In 1980 he was transferred to Mainz, West Germany (now Germany), where he was the assistant commander of a mechanized infantry division—that is, a division that uses tanks, armored personnel carriers, and other heavy vehicles. There he acquired a great deal of experience in commanding an armored, mechanized field force; a decade later, this experience would help him plan and carry out armored assaults in Operation Desert Shield and Operation Desert Storm. He earned a promotion to the two-star rank of major general in 1982, at the end of his second year in Mainz.

Schwarzkopf's European posting was followed by a 10-month stint of Pentagon duty, during which he served as the director of the army's personnel department. But in June 1983 he achieved a lifelong goal. Thirty years earlier, as a cadet at West Point, he had dreamed of being a general in command of a division. That had seemed the highest possible ambition, and now he had reached it. He was assigned to take over as commanding general of a mechanized infantry division at Fort Stewart, Georgia. But almost as soon as General Schwarzkopf had settled into his new command headquarters, he went to war again.

Schwarzkopf had gone bass fishing on a Sunday afternoon in October 1983 and came home with a good catch, promising his family that he would prepare "a beautiful Southern fried bass dinner." Just as he put the first fish in the frying pan, the telephone rang. A high-level army staff officer told him, "Don't make any plans for the next three weeks. You've been selected for a special mission." The following day, Schwarzkopf found out what the mission was: He was to serve as the senior army adviser to Vice-admiral Joseph Metcalf, a navy officer who had been given command of a top-secret operation code-named Urgent Fury. The operation was the invasion of Grenada, an island in the Caribbean Sea that was less than one-third the size of Fort Stewart. The Schwarzkopfs had to face what Norman had long ago warned Brenda might happen: "I have to go," he said, "and I can't tell you where." Although she was frightened, she tried to hide her fears from the children. She thought Norman was being sent to Lebanon, where a terrorist bomb had destroyed a U.S. Marine Corps barracks just the day before.

Unlike Lebanon, Grenada had not been in the headlines, but trouble had been brewing there for some time. Powerful factions there were friendly with the government of Cuba, a large Caribbean island that had been an outpost of communism in the Western Hemisphere for several decades. The United States worried that Cuban aid given to Grenada to build an airport was actually being used to stockpile weapons; later, in fact, a large cache of Soviet-made weapons and armored vehicles was found on the island. The United States was also concerned about a buildup of Cuban soldiers and advisers in Grenada.

Matters came to a head in October 1983, when a coup led by a military official overthrew and murdered Maurice Bishop, Grenada's prime minister, replacing him with leaders who were more hostile to the United States. The anti-Communist faction on the island appealed to the United States to intervene and prevent a Cuban takeover, and neighboring Caribbean nations indicated that they would not object to U.S. action. Furthermore, some 600 Americans were living in Grenada and attending medical school there. Metcalf was ordered to evacuate the American students from the island.

Although Urgent Fury was primarily a U.S. Navy operation, it included army troops, and Schwarzkopf was sent along to advise Metcalf on how best to use these troops. The two men got along well and Metcalf respected and

In October 1983, U.S. soldiers patrol a street in Greenville, Grenada. Schwarzkopf served as the senior army adviser for the U.S. invasion of the small island nation.

followed Schwarzkopf's advice, even in several cases in which some of his navy officers disagreed.

On his way to Grenada aboard the navy aircraft carrier *Guam*, Schwarzkopf stood alone by the rail and looked out over a turbulent sea. He wondered whether Grenada was going to become another Vietnam. "I asked myself why on earth the U.S. was getting involved in Grenada," he later remarked. "Then I said, 'Schwarzkopf, just let it sort itself out. You're an instrument of policy. You don't make policy.'" And having made that decision, he wanted to make the operation as swift and efficient as he could.

On the second day of the invasion, when he flew into Grenada, Schwarzkopf was reassured that the United States had been right to intervene. From the air he saw big red letters painted on a soccer field in the capital city of St. George. "I have seen that sign on walls all over the world—in Berlin, Vietnam, Tokyo, and even in the Pentagon," he recalls. "It always says something like 'Long Live Marxism' or 'Down with the U.S.' But as the helicopter got closer and I could read it, I saw that it said 'God Bless America.'" And a few days later, when he saw the rescued American medical students kiss the ground at a U.S. airport, he was "one hundred percent sure we did the right thing in Grenada."

The invasion of Grenada took about a week. Schwarzkopf's biggest contribution was advising Metcalf to launch an amphibious assault—sending marines ashore from ships and helicopters out at sea—on the western side of the island to rescue some soldiers who had been trapped in the governor-general's mansion. Metcalf followed this suggestion, and the maneuver succeeded.

Schwarzkopf evaluated the Grenada operation as a success for the U.S. military. The medical students were rescued, and Cuban influence on Grenada was all but eliminated. But not everything ran smoothly during the invasion, and Schwarzkopf learned two valuable lessons. The first lesson was about the importance of good intelligence, as information about the enemy and the terrain is called. The intelligence available to the U.S. forces in Grenada was badly prepared and out of date. Intelligence reports were wrong about the number and location of the American students, the number of Cuban soldiers on the island, and the Cubans' readiness to fight. Soldiers were so poorly prepared that at times they had to find their way around the island using tourist maps seized from souvenir stands. Schwarzkopf saw that first-class, up-to-date intelligence reports were vital to a smooth-running operation. During Operation Desert Storm, he would insist on having nothing but the best and most complete intelligence support.

The second lesson he learned was that no matter how much a commanding officer might dislike the idea of reporters and photographers cluttering up a combat zone, he or she was going to have to deal with the press. The Department of Defense had barred all reporters from Grenada, and Metcalf had even threatened to shoot at a group of journalists who had chartered a boat and ventured into Grenadian waters in the hope of getting a hot story. The clash turned into an angry, heated debate between the press and the military. The press resented being excluded and insisted on the public's right to know what the military was doing; the military insisted that roving reporters simply endangered themselves and others. Eventually, as a result of Operation Urgent Fury, the Pentagon and the press developed a plan for a press pool, which would give the media controlled access to some parts of combat zones. The pool system was to receive its first major test in Operation Desert Storm, and General Schwarzkopf, remembering the hostility of the press after Grenada, would work hard at maintaining a good relationship with most members of the press corps.

For Schwarzkopf, the best part of Operation Urgent Fury was the return home. After two dreary homecomings from Vietnam, he did not expect much of a welcome. But when he arrived at Fort Stewart, a small group had gathered to greet him with big Welcome Home signs and the army band. Brenda and the children were there, and so was Bear, his beloved black Labrador dog. Staff members, their wives and children, and even some of the privates from his infantry division cheered when he walked out of the airplane. He was so surprised that at first he did not realize that the welcome was for him. "But when it finally dawned on me," he told C. D. B. Bryan in 1984, "it was probably one of the greatest thrills I have ever had in my entire life." He was deeply relieved to find that although many nations had been highly critical of the invasion, the majority of the American public supported what the army had done in Grenada.

In the five years after Grenada, Schwarzkopf had four postings. First he finished his two-year tour as division commander at Fort Stewart. During this time he dedicated himself to improving his division's performance at the brand-new combat simulation center in Fort Irwin, California, where laser technology allowed soldiers to experience highly realistic mock battles. In 1985 he went back to the Pentagon once more, this time as the assistant deputy chief of staff for the army. It was a high-level position, but Schwarzkopf was as frustrated as ever with a desk job. As always during his career, his heart was out in the field with the soldiers.

His next posting took him back into the field—back to Fort Lewis in Washington State, where he commanded the

The Pentagon, located in Arlington, Virginia, houses the administrative offices of the U.S. military, including those of the Department of the Army. Schwarzkopf worked at the Pentagon from 1985 to 1986, serving as the army's assistant deputy chief of staff.

infantry corps. It was his largest command yet, and shortly after arriving at Fort Lewis in the summer of 1986, he was promoted to the rank of lieutenant general. He enjoyed being back in the Pacific Northwest, and he reflected that three decades of army life since he had left West Point had brought him, along with some suffering and confusion, a great deal of satisfaction. To his West Point classmates in their 30th-year anniversary book, he wrote, "Hang in there! The next 30 years are gonna be just as much fun as the last 30!"

In November 1988, Schwarzkopf was promoted to the rank of four-star general. He was also named commander in chief of United States Central Command, the command unit that is responsible for U.S. military operations in most of the Middle East.

He was at Fort Lewis for only a year, and by August 1987 he had moved across the country again to take up another staff position. He was now the U.S. Army's deputy chief of staff at the Pentagon, but he had a second job at the same time, serving as the senior army member of the U.S. Military Staff Committee at the United Nations. This responsibility brought him into contact with dignitaries and officials from many nations and helped polish his diplomatic skills. A few years later, he would draw upon this experience in international diplomacy when he became responsible for maintaining good relations among the representatives of the 28 nations that formed the allied coalition in Operation Desert Storm.

In November 1988, after 32 years in the army and 25 postings on 3 continents, Norman Schwarzkopf became a 4-star general. He also received a new and challenging assignment as commander in chief of United States Central Command in Tampa, Florida. While his family moved into a two-story, four-bedroom, white-stucco house and went about the familiar routine of settling into a new town, General Schwarzkopf took control of Central Command, or CentCom. Not long after he took command, he announced plans to retire in 3 years, after 35 years of service. He had no idea how eventful those three years were to be. In taking charge of CentCom, Schwarzkopf had inherited the military responsibility for one of the world's most troubled and volatile regions.

Schwarzkopf and King Fahd of Saudi Arabia review coalition troops on January 6, 1991. After Iraq's army invaded and occupied Kuwait, the United States and other nations sent troops to Saudi Arabia to protect that country from a possible Iraqi invasion.

6

A Line in the Sand

CENTCOM IS ONE OF SEVERAL JOINT COMMANDS set up by the Department of Defense to coordinate U.S. military preparedness and activity in various parts of the world. In that respect, it is like the European Command and the Pacific Command, drawing together representatives of the different armed forces. Unlike these commands, however, CentCom has no bases in the part of the world for which it is responsible. That region of responsibility covers 19 nations, stretching for more than 3,000 miles from Egypt, Sudan, and Kenya in northeast Africa to Afghanistan and Pakistan in south Asia. Although CentCom does not include Israel, Syria, or Lebanon, it does include the rest of the Middle East: Jordan, Saudi Arabia, Iraq, Iran, and the smaller Persian Gulf nations.

The unique problem faced by CentCom commanders is that the United States has not been able to establish permanent military bases in the command's region of operation. CentCom is entitled to call upon U.S. Army, Navy, Air Force, and Marine Corps troops that are stationed in other parts of the world if it needs to send a field force into action, but because it has no bases in its area of responsibility, the command has been regarded by some critics as a useless, helpless bureaucracy. In the wake of Norman Schwarzkopf and Operation Desert Storm, however, that opinion is no longer widely held.

When Schwarzkopf became commander in chief, or CINC, of CentCom, he took over a staff of about 700 officers and enlisted men and women from all four armed forces. Their job was o study reports about events in their region, evaluate how those events might affect U.S. interests there, and develop plans to deal with any crises that might occur. CentCom staff members formed a favorable impression of their new CINC, who walked around headquarters introducing himself to everyone, asking where they were from, and generally establishing a friendly presence. They soon learned to be wary of his outbursts of temper, but they also discovered that he was quick to apologize for losing his temper. And he always made it clear what he expected from people so that they would be able to perform well. Lieutenant General Joseph Hoar, Schwarzkopf's chief of staff at CentCom, has said, "I never worked for a guy who was more clear in giving guidance on what he wanted."

As CINC of CentCom, Schwarzkopf made several visits to countries in his region. He got along well with the Muslim rulers of Saudi Arabia, gladly joining their hunting excursions into the desert and wearing their traditional long robe for a ceremonial dinner. He enjoyed revisiting the part of the world where his father had been stationed during the 1940s. But he was unable to visit Iran, which had turned violently against the United States in 1979 when the shah was overthrown. Islamic fundamentalists had assumed control of the government and proclaimed their intent to eliminate all Western influence from Iran.

Iran and its neighbor Iraq were locked in a bitter, devastatingly destructive war from 1980 to 1988, and almost all

In May 1987, smoke billows from the USS Stark *after it was struck by an Exocet missile launched by Iraq. Saddam Hussein apologized for the firing of the rocket, which killed 37 members of the ship's crew.*

U.S. military activity in the CentCom region in the late 1980s had centered on this war. Although the United States did not interfere directly in the conflict, it sent warships to the Persian Gulf to protect the oil tankers of many countries. On several occasions the U.S. fleet was involved in hostilities. In 1987 the USS *Stark* was struck by a missile fired from an Iraqi plane, and 37 American servicemen were killed. Saddam Hussein, the leader of Iraq, apologized to Washington and claimed that the firing was an accident. In 1988 the USS *Vincennes*, a missile cruiser engaged in a skirmish with Iranian gunboats, shot down an Iranian airliner, killing all 290 civilians aboard; the radar operators had confused the airliner with a fighter plane. By the time Schwarzkopf came to CentCom, these and other recent incidents in the gulf region had increased tensions and created a sense of impending confrontation.

One of Schwarzkopf's duties as CINC of CentCom was to report each year to the Senate Armed Services Committee about possible threats to U.S. interests in his region. In his first briefing to the committee, in March 1989, he repeated a view that had been held by strategists for the previous 40 years: that the Soviet Union, which had long wished for a warm-water port on the Persian Gulf, posed the greatest threat to the stability of the CentCom region.

Schwarzkopf felt that, with a few exceptions, the United States had not been effective in making allies in the region, and that the Soviet Union was ready to increase its influence in Africa, the Middle East, and Asia. He added that Iraq was "a potential threat" to the smaller and weaker Persian Gulf nations. Although Iraq had suffered considerable damage in its long war with Iran, it had emerged with a large military force still intact. Saddam Hussein had hinted on many occasions that he might turn against his Arab neighbors, even though they had given him billions of dollars' worth of aid during his war with Iran.

In 1990, when General Schwarzkopf gave his next Senate committee briefing, he held different views. He believed that the Soviet threat to the CentCom region was greatly reduced. The previous year had brought sweeping changes to the world, including the fall of many Soviet-backed Communist governments in Eastern Europe and the rise of serious political and economic trouble within the Soviet Union. Internal problems were likely to keep the Soviets busy, and besides, the United States had started to move away from the position that the Soviet Union was automatically and inevitably the enemy of U.S. interests. Instead, Schwarzkopf told the Senate committee, the greatest threat to the CentCom region now came from local conflicts that could lead to a regional war. Such a war would upset the balance of power throughout the Middle East and also threaten the world's supply of oil, much of which comes from the Middle East. Schwarzkopf felt that the country most likely to start a war was Iraq.

In late July 1990 the U.S. Central Intelligence Agency (CIA) received satellite photographs that showed a buildup of Iraqi troops on Iraq's border with Kuwait, a small country sandwiched between Saudi Arabia, Iraq, and the Persian Gulf. The CIA passed this information to the White House, which in turn passed it to Kuwait. They all decided that Saddam Hussein was bluffing. He would not invade Kuwait—at least not this year.

Schwarzkopf was not so sure. He feared that Hussein might indeed launch an attack upon wealthy but poorly defended Kuwait. Iraq had long been greedy for a larger share of the profits from the Rumaila oil field, a petroleum-producing region that straddles the border between the two countries. Or Hussein might try to seize Warba and Bubiyan, two Kuwaiti islands in the Persian Gulf that block Iraq's coastline.

Earlier in July, Schwarzkopf had organized CentCom's annual computer war-game training exercise, and 350 members of his staff carried it out. The exercise, which was called Internal Look 90, started with the premise that Iraq had invaded Kuwait. Each staff member had to respond as though such an invasion had really taken place. The point of the exercise was to see whether CentCom's staff could handle the organizational and communications challenge. What troops would they order to the region, and how would the troops get there? Where would supplies come from? What sort of a command system could be set up?

On August 1, four days after the war game ended, Schwarzkopf finished a workout on the exercise equipment he keeps in his garage at home. He was headed for the shower when the special telephone that is his hot line to the Pentagon rang. The voice on the other end belonged to General Colin Powell, the chairman of the U.S. Joint Chiefs of Staff and Schwarzkopf's immediate boss. Powell said, "Well, they've crossed." Schwarzkopf knew what Powell meant: Iraqi troops had crossed the Kuwaiti border. He wondered whether it was going to be a full-fledged invasion or simply a quick run to the Rumaila oil field. Before long Powell called again. "We have reports that they're in downtown Kuwait City," he said. Schwarzkopf had his answer. It was an invasion.

Fortunately, he had a response plan ready. Internal Look 90 became the first draft of the military operation that the White House later called Operation Desert Shield.

Schwarzkopf was summoned to Washington to join Powell at a National Security Council meeting with President George Bush.

Iraq's invasion of Kuwait took less than a day. Emir al-Sabah, the ruler of Kuwait, fled the country ahead of Iraq's advancing troops. When Kuwait was completely occupied, Hussein annexed it, declaring that it was now a province of Iraq. Thousands of Kuwaiti citizens jammed the country's border, fleeing to neighboring Saudi Arabia; many of those who remained were subjected to brutal atrocities or suffered from food shortages. In addition, thousands of foreigners were trapped inside Iraq and Kuwait. Three thousand were Americans. Although Bush tried to avoid using the word *hostage*, there was considerable fear that these people would be taken prisoner and would become victims of Hussein's cruelty. Over the coming months, however, they were released.

Both Kuwait and the much larger country of Saudi Arabia, which has a long border with Iraq, are considered friends of the United States; they are the best disposed toward the United States of any of the Arab countries. Although the United States was distressed by the invasion of Kuwait, it was even more concerned that Hussein might use Kuwait as a base for attacking Saudi Arabia's Gulf coast. If Hussein succeeded in taking over all or part of Saudi Arabia, he could become the wealthiest and most powerful ruler in the Persian Gulf. He would control a great share of the world's largest oil reserve—and he would most definitely not be a friend of the United States. From the moment of invasion, then, the United States had two clear goals: to prevent Iraq from invading Saudi Arabia and to cause Iraq to withdraw from Kuwait. The question was whether or not the United States was willing to go to war to achieve these goals. President Bush felt from the start that it would be necessary to use force. Soon after the invasion, General Powell advised Bush to "draw a line in the sand"—in effect, to tell Hussein that he would

The Persian Gulf Region

be met with force if he tried to cross the Saudi border. On August 8, Bush declared that the line had been drawn.

At the same time, the United Nations (UN) condemned Iraq's act of aggression against a peaceful neighbor nation and ordered economic sanctions and a naval embargo against Iraq. In nations that supported the UN move, Iraqi investments and bank accounts were frozen, the sale of goods to Iraq was cut off, and the purchase of Iraqi goods, including oil, was halted. The naval blockade in the Persian Gulf kept Iraq isolated. The sanctions did not cause Hussein to withdraw from Kuwait, although some observers felt that the sanctions might work if they were allowed to stand for many months. The UN did, however, authorize its member nations to use force against Iraq if Iraq did not withdraw voluntarily from Kuwait.

Meanwhile, Schwarzkopf accompanied Secretary of Defense Richard Cheney to Jidda, Saudi Arabia, to meet with that country's King Fahd. They told him that the

On August 6, 1990, the United Nations Security Council votes to implement sweeping trade and military sanctions against Iraq as a direct response to Iraq's invasion of Kuwait.

United States was willing to send troops to defend Saudi Arabia from Iraq, and that it would withdraw those troops whenever requested to do so. After some uncertainty, King Fahd replied, "We want you to come." Schwarzkopf points out that this was a courageous and difficult decision for Fahd because Saudi Arabia, like most Middle Eastern nations, has a strict policy against allowing foreign countries to build military bases on its soil. The United States, in particular, was disliked by some traditional Saudis, who felt that Americans were disrespectful of Arab and Muslim cultures. There was a chance that Fahd's people, or the other Arab nations in the region, would turn against him if he accepted U.S. help. But Hussein must have seemed a bigger threat than the United States, for most of the Arab world stood behind Fahd.

President Bush ordered 125,000 troops to the Persian Gulf and asked other nations to join the United States and Saudi Arabia in a coalition, or unified front, against Iraq. Twenty-eight nations responded. Some were Arab states such as Qatar and Egypt—and even Syria, which had been opposed to the United States for a long time. Others were traditional Western allies: the United Kingdom, France, Italy. Some nations, such as Germany and Japan, were prohibited by their constitutions from sending troops but promised to pay a share of the cost of assembling the coalition force. The defensive operation that began to take shape on the eastern Arabian sands was called Operation Desert Shield. The person responsible for turning Desert Shield from a plan into a reality was General Norman Schwarzkopf.

He headed the largest, fastest, farthest-reaching deployment of military forces in U.S. history. A steady stream of orders began flowing out of CentCom headquarters, covering everything from troop allocations to transport and communications equipment to the shipment of supplies. Because the troops were not going to an existing base, barracks of some sort would have to be constructed. Tanks,

U.S. troops arrive in Saudi Arabia in August 1990 at the beginning of Operation Desert Shield. By the end of August, 100,000 U.S. troops were stationed in Saudi Arabia. The number of troops under Schwarzkopf's command would eventually total 675,000—the largest field force since World War II.

trucks, food, uniforms, munitions, desert survival equipment, medical facilities—all would have to be found, transported to Saudi Arabia, stored, and distributed. Although Schwarzkopf's primary responsibility was the strategic planning of possible military engagements and the deployment of troops, he and his staff were ultimately accountable for making sure that the myriad of vitally important details were properly handled.

By the end of August, the United States had sent about 100,000 troops to Saudi Arabia. More were on the way, and troops from the international coalition soon began arriving as well. Eventually the number of troops under Schwarzkopf's command was to total 675,000—the largest field force since World War II. Part of Schwarzkopf's job as commander of the operation was to direct the activities of the other countries' forces without appearing too dominating. Although he had good working relationships with the foreign officers, the task involved a considerable exercise of diplomacy.

Schwarzkopf remained at CentCom headquarters in Tampa until August 25, when he flew to Riyadh, the capital of Saudi Arabia, and established himself in the headquarters that his aides had set up for him in the Saudi Ministry of Defense. That day he was supposed to have driven Jessica, his younger daughter, to her first day of college, and soon afterward he was to have gone on a fishing trip with Christian. He told his family that he would make up the time with them as soon as he could.

Over the following five months, General Norman Schwarzkopf became an increasingly familiar figure on U.S. television newscasts. Clad in desert camouflage battle fatigues, wearing black metal generals' stars on his collar and a wristwatch on both wrists so that he could tell local time and Washington, D.C., time, he gave numerous interviews to the reporters who made up the media pool in Riyadh. Aware that the press chafed at military restrictions on war news, he held frequent briefings and tried to keep

Schwarzkopf invites another question during a press briefing in Riyadh, Saudi Arabia. The general became a familiar face on television in the United States, impressing many viewers with his straightforward, no-nonsense manner.

the journalists on his side by dealing with them in a straightforward, even blunt, manner.

At times Schwarzkopf was surprisingly candid. Once he told a group of reporters that he hated war. "Every waking and sleeping moment," he said, "my nightmare is the fact that I will give an order that will cause countless numbers of human beings to lose their lives. I don't want my troops to die. I don't want my troops to be maimed. It's an intensely personal, emotional thing for me. Any decision

Troops from the U.S. First Cavalry conduct an exercise march in November 1990. Near the end of 1990, Schwarzkopf began formulating plans to drive the Iraqis out of Kuwait.

that you have to make that involves the loss of human life is nothing you do lightly. I agonize over it." The public liked seeing this emotional side of the big bear of a general, but some officers felt that Schwarzkopf had become a little *too* emotional, possibly giving the impression of hesitation or confusion. Powell called Schwarzkopf and suggested that he be a little less personal in future interviews.

As 1990 drew to a close, the focus of Operation Desert Shield shifted away from defense and to offense. Once it became fairly certain that Hussein was not going to order a large-scale invasion of Saudi Arabia, the allied coalition began formulating plans to drive him out of Kuwait, under the terms of the UN resolution that authorized them to use force.

In January 1991, Sheridan tanks from the U.S. 82nd Airborne Division move across the Saudi desert during maneuvers as the UN deadline for Iraq to withdraw from Kuwait approaches.

Schwarzkopf knew that he would need many more troops to launch a successful campaign against the Iraqi army. He was not about to make the same mistakes that had been made in Vietnam because of lack of full commitment. He told Powell and Bush that if he went on the offensive he wanted to hit hard and fast, with all the power he could muster. In October he requested more aircraft carriers, more armored divisions, and more Marine Corps support. He also told Powell that he needed until January 15 to get his force prepared for the start of a shooting war.

Bush approved the request, and by November the second phase of the buildup was under way. Secretary of State James Baker got the use-of-force resolution approved by the UN Security Council, with a deadline of January 15 for Iraq's withdrawal. But in the final days of 1990 and the first days of 1991, Hussein sat tight in Baghdad, the capital of Iraq, and his troops showed no sign of moving from Kuwait. General Schwarzkopf told his family to save his Christmas presents until he could open them at home, and the world waited in suspense, excitement, and dread for the fighting to start. Operation Desert Shield was about to make way for Operation Desert Storm.

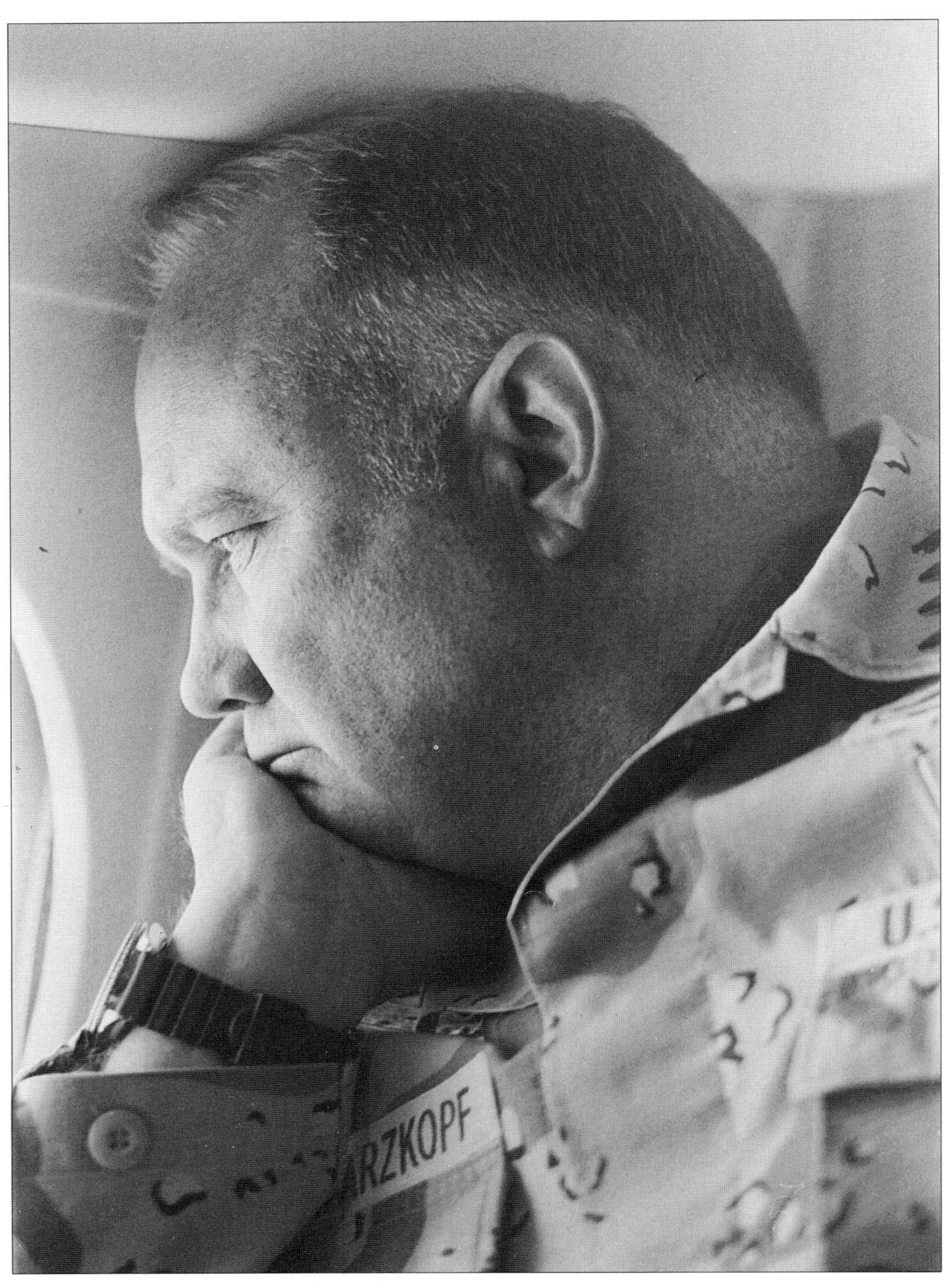

Schwarzkopf spends a pensive moment during a flight on January 13, 1991. The general was flying to several bases in Saudi Arabia to inspect his troops.

7

Desert Storm

PRESIDENT GEORGE BUSH HAD DEFIED SADDAM HUSSEIN to cross the "line in the sand," but in the end it was Bush who crossed the line—or the U.S. and allied air and ground troops that crossed it for him. Hussein did not invade Saudi Arabia, but neither did he withdraw from Kuwait. The January 15 deadline came and went. Then, early in the morning of January 17, the war began. The coalition forces attacked Iraq. It was a solemn moment, not a jubilant one, for Supreme Allied Commander Schwarzkopf and his aides in their war room deep below the Ministry of Defense. As the first Apache helicopters crossed Iraq's border and approached their targets, the commander and his staff joined in a short prayer for the safety of the troops. Schwarzkopf then played a tape of one of his favorite songs, "God Bless the U.S.A.," by Lee Greenwood.

The war started as an air war, consisting of sorties, or bombing runs, over Iraqi territory. The skill and bravery of the allied pilots was beyond question, but part of the credit for the allied victory must go to

On January 17, 1991, rounds of antiaircraft artillery light up the night sky over Baghdad as the Persian Gulf war begins. Coalition forces conducted more than 1,000 bombing sorties against targets in Iraq and Kuwait during the first 24 hours of the war.

the very sophisticated military technology they had at their disposal. In addition to the huge, heavy B-52 bomber and the low-flying A-10 Thunderbolt attack bomber (called the Warthog because of the distinctive profile provided by the cannon mounted on its nose), air power included the F-117A Stealth bomber, invisible to enemy radar; the Apache helicopter, capable of firing laser-guided missiles; and AWACs and F4-G Wild Weasels, which have electronic gear that can jam enemy radar. When it came to bombs, the allies had the Tomahawk cruise missile, which is launched from a ship. Reaching speeds of 885 miles per hour, the Tomahawk uses a computer to match the terrain it flies over with a programmed electronic map that guides it to its target. They had the Patriot missile, which was used to blast Iraq's Scud missiles out of the sky over Israel and Saudi Arabia. And they had an array of guidance systems that used laser beams and television to guide "smart bombs" with pinpoint accuracy. One widely broadcast image showed a Tomahawk gliding straight toward impact with the roof of Baghdad's central telephone and communications building. Another smart bomb was photographed zipping through the doorway of an Iraqi command post.

The air war was a disaster for Iraq. In 6 weeks, the allies made more than 100,000 sorties over Iraq. Most of Hussein's aircraft were destroyed, although more than 100 of his best planes fled to Iran. Hussein hoped that he could save them to fight at a later date, but Iran's president Hashemi Rafsanjani impounded the planes, saying that he would return them to Iraq when the war was over. Iraq fired 81 Scuds into Israel and Saudi Arabia, but few of them did any real damage. On the other hand, hundreds of Iraqi tanks, missile launchers, and troop carriers were destroyed, as were bridges, telecommunications lines, airfields, and roads.

Schwarzkopf consistently refused to estimate enemy casualties. He felt that such estimates were a poor gauge of the status of the war and were reminiscent of the dubious "body counts" of Vietnam. Still, military observers placed Iraqi casualties at about 50,000, although some other sources claim that the death toll may be up to three times higher. Some of these deaths occurred in the final few days of the war, when the allies made a ground assault on Kuwait and Iraq. U.S. casualties in the war were fewer than 150; the allied total was 263. Except for a brief and insignificant occupation of the Saudi town of al-Khafji, not far from the Kuwait border, Iraq's forces achieved no penetration into Saudi Arabia.

In late February, in the fifth week of the air war, President Bush, with the support of the other coalition nations,

On January 14, 1991, Iraqis watch Saddam Hussein give a televised speech in which he urges Iraq's to fight to the death to hold on to Kuwait. When asked about Hussein's military acumen, Schwarzkopf retorted, "He is neither a strategist, nor is he schooled in the operational art, nor is he a tactician, nor is he a general, nor is he a soldier."

offered Hussein a chance to withdraw. Hussein ignored the offer. Bush then instructed Schwarzkopf, his field commander, to liberate Kuwait.

Schwarzkopf had been ready for that order for weeks. As soon as the air strikes had begun on January 17, he had secretly sent a large allied force north and west, across the border and into the center of Iraq. By keeping a massive concentration of troops near Kuwait and the southeastern border of Iraq, he made Hussein believe that the allied attack would come from that direction—from the Persian Gulf. But when he gave the word to launch the ground attack on February 24, Schwarzkopf sent the western wing up and around Hussein's unprotected, neglected flank and then straight toward Baghdad to attack the unsuspecting Iraqi army from the rear. At the same time, a direct assault on Iraqi forces along the Kuwait border, accompanied by heavy air strikes, drove the Iraqi occupying forces back toward their own border.

Hussein's troops were caught off guard by the flanking maneuver, which Schwarzkopf referred to in one of his press briefings as similar to the Hail Mary maneuver in football. The Iraqi army was large—about 1 million strong by most estimates—but it was poorly equipped, demoral-

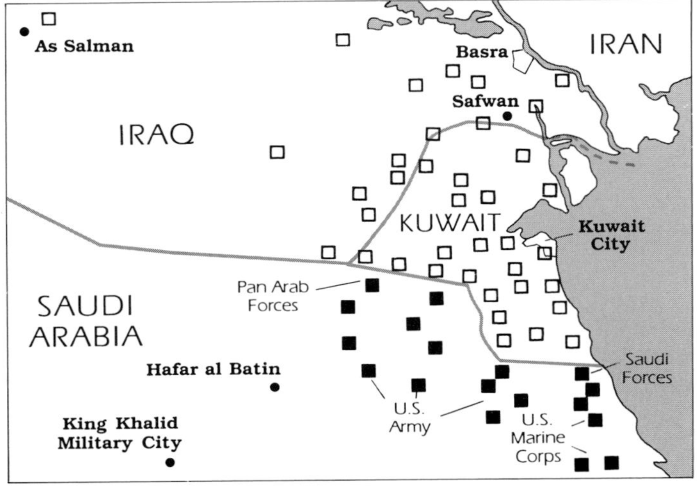

Beginning on August 3, 1990, coalition forces under the command of General Norman Schwarzkopf positioned themselves in Saudi Arabia along the Kuwaiti border. The troops maintained their defensive stance until January 1991.

ized, and not very willing to stand and fight. As many as 60,000 Iraqi soldiers surrendered peacefully, even eagerly, in some cases, to the allies. After the war ended they were returned to Iraq.

The ground war lasted four days. On February 27, 100 hours after Schwarzkopf launched the ground assault, the Iraqis were in complete rout. Kuwait had been liberated. Yet Saddam Hussein was still in power in Baghdad. There were those in the military and in the American public who felt that the coalition should simply make a clean sweep of it, continue with a full invasion of Iraq, and overturn Hussein's government. There is no doubt that Schwarzkopf's field force could have done just that if those had been his orders. But President Bush decided to end the fighting when the initial goal had been met. "Kuwait is liberated," he announced. "Iraq's army is defeated. Our military objectives are met." The president ordered the coalition to suspend the offensive until terms of a cease-fire could be worked out.

Schwarzkopf has been careful to point out that he is a soldier, not a policymaker. Only once did he slip and reveal that he wished the victory over Hussein could have been more complete—he remarked that he had been "prevented

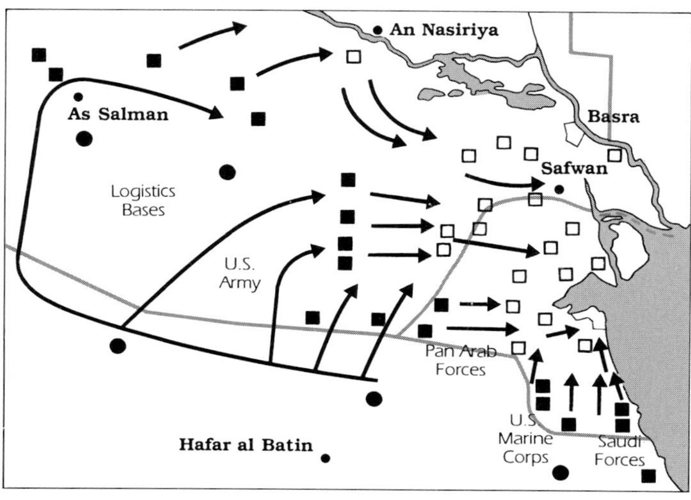

Between January 16 and February 23, 1991, most of the coalition forces shifted west to outflank Iraq's fortified positions. At 4:00 A.M. on February 24, Saudi troops and U.S. Marines thrust north toward Kuwait City. Coalition forces stationed in the west charged behind Iraqi lines, cutting off escape routes.

After punching through Iraq's defensive lines, an engineering squad from the U.S. Army's First Infantry Division races past a burning oil well on its way toward Kuwait City. Coalition forces liberated Kuwait on February 27, 1991.

from finishing" the job. Afterward he realized that the comment would be interpreted as criticism of Bush, and he promptly apologized to the president. "The president told me to forget all about it," a smiling Schwarzkopf said to reporters. "The guy's my boss, and when he tells me to forget about it, I'm gonna forget about it."

On March 3, 1991, Schwarzkopf and the highest-ranking Saudi, Kuwaiti, French, and British officials met with Iraqi officials in a tent at the airfield of Safwan, Iraq. There they negotiated an agreement to the terms under which the allies would halt their attack on Iraq. The Iraqis promised to release allied prisoners of war, to accept the UN resolutions, and to reveal the location of all land and sea mines that they had planted in Kuwait. Another of the allied terms was that no aircraft could fly in Iraqi airspace. The Iraqis asked Schwarzkopf if they could use their helicopters to carry government officials from place to place on peaceful missions, as most roads and bridges had been destroyed. He agreed, thinking the request harmless. Later, when he learned that the Iraqi army was using the helicopters as gunships to put down rebel uprisings against Hussein, Schwarzkopf said bitterly that the Iraqis had "suckered" him.

Iraq's internal politics were gravely disrupted by the war. Saddam Hussein, who had promised his people that he would lead Iraq to victory over the United States in "the mother of all battles," had instead taken a sound and costly thrashing. Many observers, including Schwarzkopf, believed that if the allies did not kill him then someone among the Iraqis would do so, and the United States went so far as to utter words of encouragement to rebel factions within Iraq that staged uprisings against Hussein. Two of the biggest uprisings involved the Shiites, a minority Muslim sect, and the Kurds, an ethnic group distributed throughout the mountains of southern Turkey, northeastern Iraq, and northwestern Iran.

In the immediate aftermath of the war, it seemed that these rebellions might succeed in toppling Hussein from power. Soon, though, he gathered the surviving members of his government and other supporters around him and began striking out at the rebels, sending army and police units into the countryside to attack them. The rebels became refugees, swarming to the borders in a desperate attempt to get out of Iraq. The plight of the Kurdish refugees, whole villages of whom were stranded in the cold mountain passes on the Turkish-Iraqi border, attracted worldwide attention. International relief efforts began taking food, water, and medicine to the refugees; among the relief workers were soldiers from the allied coalition. When the United Nations criticized Iraq's treatment of the Kurds, Hussein invited the Kurds to return home without fear of punishment. Months later, however, many of them were still in refugee camps, hoping to be allowed to enter some other country.

Although the defeat inflicted on Hussein by the allies was so complete that it amounted to an utter rout, he had managed several last-minute strikes of his own. The allies had greatly feared that he would use chemical or biological weapons, such as poison gas, for he was widely believed to control stockpiles of such weapons. No chemical or biological weapons were unleashed, however. But on Hussein's order the Iraqi forces carried out monstrous acts of what Schwarzkopf called "environmental terrorism." First they drained five Kuwaiti oil tankers into the waters of the Persian Gulf and opened the pipes of Kuwait's largest oil terminal into the sea, creating an immense, deliberate oil spill. Experts say that the Persian Gulf oil spill amounted to about 1.5 million gallons, making it the biggest spill in history. (By comparison, the Exxon *Valdez* spilled about 260,000 gallons of oil in Alaska's Prince William Sound in March 1989.)

Newsreel footage showed greasy black scum along miles of the Persian Gulf shoreline, with cormorants and other seabirds floundering helplessly in the muck. Schwarzkopf, a lover of scuba diving, fishing, and the outdoors, was saddened by this threat to the region's

Grounded on the Saudi shore, an oil-enshrouded cormorant awaits its death. Schwarzkopf publicly condemned Iraq for engaging in acts of environmental terrorism, such as opening a large oil pipe at a Kuwaiti refinery that spewed thousands of barrels of oil into the Persian Gulf.

Iraqi soldiers surrender to U.S. troops on February 27, 1991. After spending six months billeted in foxholes and reinforced bunkers, the Iraqi ground forces offered little resistance to coalition ground forces.

marine ecology and to its fishing industry. Not all of the spill came from Hussein's eco-sabotage, though; 20 to 30 percent of it was caused by allied bombing of coastal targets.

Hussein's second act of environmental terrorism has had even more widespread results. In what appears to have been sheer spite and hatefulness, he ordered his retreating troops to set Kuwait's oil wells on fire. More than a quarter of the country's 1,000 or so wells were ignited, sending huge, dense plumes of oily smoke high into the atmosphere. Months after the end of the war, many of the fires had still not been brought under control, and the resultant atmospheric pollution will likely affect the world's climate and air quality for many years to come. Some weather scientists fear that the massive clouds of smoke could alter patterns of wind and rainfall across much of Asia, possibly leading to drought and famine in India and other nations.

Throughout the months of Desert Shield and the weeks of Desert Storm, General Schwarzkopf had lived on a demanding schedule. His personal billet was a room in the complex warren underneath the Saudi Ministry of

On March 3, 1991, Schwarzkopf meets with Iraqi officers (right) to negotiate the terms of a cease-fire.

Defense. In it he kept pictures of his family, a toy bear sent to him by his sister Sally, his cross-country ski exercise machine, a camouflage-covered Bible, a set of videotapes of the PBS Civil War TV series, and—next to his bed in case of emergency—a shotgun. He spent relatively little time in this chamber, however. His workday averaged 18 hours.

At 7:00 A.M. each day he held a staff briefing, reviewing every event of the past 24 hours with his staff. At 10:00 A.M. he held a coalition meeting, attended by the senior officers of the other countries' forces, to make plans and share information. At 7:00 P.M. he held a command meeting with the top officers of the U.S. Army, Navy, Air Force, and Marine Corps field forces in his command. He periodically went across the street to the Hyatt Regency Hotel, which had been turned into the press headquarters of Riyadh, for briefings or interviews with the media pool. He talked on the phone with General Powell almost every day, sometimes three or four times a day. He tried to call home twice a week, too, so that he could have a few words with Brenda and the children.

When he was able to get away from the war room and the rest of command headquarters for a few hours, General

Schwarzkopf would venture out for a look at the troops—something he always wished he could do more often. These were not carefree, spontaneous jaunts. Everywhere he went he was accompanied by Special Forces bodyguards and elite Saudi security guards as a protection against terrorism or an assassination attempt. He was also accompanied by his aides, including a sergeant who carried a 60-pound satellite hookup so that Schwarzkopf could be in instant contact with Washington at any moment. Despite these rather cumbersome precautions, he reveled in his opportunities to visit the field and mingle with the troops, often pausing to ask a soldier where he or she was from and to say, "You're doing a great job. Glad you're here!"

Schwarzkopf had left Tampa for Saudi Arabia in August 1990 not knowing how long he might be away from home or what form the crisis in Kuwait would take. Like every military man or woman who serves overseas in combat, he was looking forward to going home. But the end of the fighting did not mean a return to the United States for everyone. Although some troops were able to go home immediately, many others had to remain in the Gulf region for a "mopping up" period. Schwarzkopf stayed on the job for two months after the fighting stopped. In April he was able to turn the final phases of the mopping up over to subordinate officers and climb aboard a military jet for the flight to Tampa.

This flight was the fourth homecoming from war of his army career. But this time, his reception was to be unlike anything he had ever experienced.

The face of this Kurdish refugee reflects the anguish of the Iraqi Kurds after their rebellion against Hussein's regime failed. Nearly 850,000 refugees fled to the mountains of northern Iraq when the remnants of Hussein's army quashed the Kurdish insurrection in late March 1991.

On April 22, 1991, admirers welcome Schwarzkopf upon his return to MacDill Air Force Base in Tampa, Florida. After spending 239 days overseas, the general was elated to be reunited with his family.

8

The Hero's Welcome

IN THE SPRING OF 1990, General Norman Schwarzkopf had been respected and admired within the army and almost unknown outside it. A year later, he was an American hero. But he was not the only new hero. The outpouring of support and affection for the Desert Storm troops was the exact opposite of the scorn and disapproval that had been shown to so many returning Vietnam veterans.

During operations Desert Shield and Desert Storm, the United States seemed to burst forth in yellow ribbons and bows, adopted as symbols of support for the soldiers in Saudi Arabia. They appeared on lapel buttons and bumper stickers, on storefronts and shirtfronts, on trees and flagpoles and municipal water towers. Even those who opposed the war were careful to say that they meant no criticism of the individual soldiers.

Although there was an antiwar movement during Operation Desert Storm, it never achieved the dimensions of the Vietnam era antiwar movement. After the air war started, several peace marches in

Washington, D.C., drew large crowds of antiwar demonstrators. One big antiwar protest in San Francisco resulted in the arrest of 1,000 activists. But public opinion polls showed that most Americans felt that both the policymakers and the soldiers were doing the right thing.

Schwarzkopf reported that this almost universal agreement reached the combat zone in the form of hundreds of thousands of cards and letters to the men and women at the front. This created feelings in the soldiers that were quite different from the isolation and despair that many Vietnam soldiers had felt. "They feel good about what they're doing over here," he said of his troops. "And there's no question but that the reason they feel that way is because they know they have the support of the overwhelming majority of the American people."

The American people had also gotten to know General Schwarzkopf through interviews and televised broadcasts of his press briefings, particularly his lengthy, emotional briefing on February 27, the day the war ended. The public was captivated by Schwarzkopf's boyish grin, by his obvious strength and uprightness, and by the passionate commitment that he showed for his soldiers' well-being. Some questions were raised, however, about the ways in which Schwarzkopf in particular and the military in general had controlled and manipulated the flow of information during the war.

The media played a curious role in Operation Desert Storm. On the one hand, the conflict was the most thoroughly recorded war in history. The Cable News Network (CNN) broadcast war news around the clock, including live reports by CNN newsman Peter Arnett from Baghdad. Television viewers saw remarkable scenes from the war, such as Patriot missiles blowing up Scuds above Riyadh or smart bombs making precise hits on their targets.

On the other hand, there were important aspects of the war that were scarcely reported at all because of the

On May 8, 1991, Schwarzkopf addresses Congress during a ceremony in his honor. The general said that his forces won the Persian Gulf war largely because of support from the American public and "the finest military equipment in the world." Speaker of the House Thomas Foley looks on.

military restrictions on where reporters could go and what they could say. Critics of the government's media policy have pointed out, for example, that the American public saw very few images of dead and wounded Iraqis or of the destruction caused by the allied bombing. Even critics of

From the visitors' gallery of the House Chamber, the Schwarzkopf family—(left to right) Jessica, Brenda, Christian, and Cynthia—applaud Norman's speech to Congress.

the way the military handled the media, however, admit that General Schwarzkopf made a good impression on the press and the public. By the time he returned to the United States, he was perhaps the most popular individual in the country.

A brass band and a crowd of well-wishers greeted him when he stepped off the plane at MacDill Air Force Base in Tampa, Florida. With tears in his eyes, he wrapped his family in a bear hug, listened to the national anthem, and declared, "It's a great day to be a soldier." Other, more lavish honors awaited. He was thanked by the president in a speech to Congress. In May he was made an honorary knight commander by Queen Elizabeth II of Great Britain. In June he was part of a huge ticker-tape parade in New

York City. Everywhere he went, people clamored for his autograph. Books and magazine articles about him appeared on every newsstand. Literary and movie agents talked excitedly about the vast sums he could earn for his memoirs, until June 1991, when he ended speculation by signing a contract to write his autobiography for Bantam Books, reportedly for more than $5 million. Corporate executives said that he could earn even more in private industry.

People began to speculate about whether the 56-year-old general might be interested in a political career; perhaps even the White House could be within his reach. Schwarzkopf claims that he has no political ambitions—but he adds that he might develop them if the right opportunity arose. "The things I feel very strongly about," he says, "are education, the war on drugs, the environment and conservation and wildlife."

Throughout the hoopla, Schwarzkopf kept his sense of perspective by remembering a scene from the movie *Patton*, which told the story of a great U.S. Army general from an earlier generation. A scene in the movie recalls a custom of the ancient Romans: Whenever a general came home victorious from the battlefield, a slave was assigned to follow him in his triumphal processions and, every so often, murmur in his ear, "Remember, you are mortal."

Schwarzkopf's greatest joy in returning to the United States was in being reunited with his wife and children. He opened his Christmas presents, ate meals of all his favorite foods, made plans to go fishing and hunting with his son, and spent hours talking and relaxing with his family. He also announced that his plans to retire on August 31, 1991, were unchanged. Having just fought and won the swiftest, most decisive war in U.S. history, he said that his new goal was "to be one of the world's great salmon fishermen."

Whatever path he follows after leaving the U.S. Army, Norman Schwarzkopf has earned a place in military history. But he has claimed a place in America's folk history as well, by giving the nation a new kind of war hero, one who possesses a keen mind, courage, a tender heart, and a warm sense of humor. His career has spanned the worst and the best American military experiences of modern times. By becoming a focus for America's patriotic pride and a symbol of honor in a military uniform, he has helped heal the wounds that the nation and the army have carried since the Vietnam War. That, as much as for his vital role in Operation Desert Storm, is why he will be remembered.

In May 1991, Schwarzkopf leads his troops in a welcome-home parade in Washington, D.C.

Further Reading

Anderson, Jack, and Dale van Atta. *Stormin' Norman: An American Hero*. New York: Zebra, 1991.

Barry, John. "A Textbook Victory." *Newsweek* (March 11, 1991): 38–40.

Benson, Harry, and Edward Barnes. "Holding the Line." *Life* (October 1990): 24–28.

Birnbaum, Jesse, and Dan Fischer. "Stormin' Norman on Top." *Time* (February 4, 1991): 28–30.

Bryan, C. D. B. *Friendly Fire*. New York: Putnam, 1976.

———. "Operation Desert Norm." *New Republic* (March 11, 1991): 20–27.

Chesnoff, Richard Z. "How the Top Cop in the Gulf Sees His Job." *U.S. News & World Report* (October 1, 1990): 34–35.

Galloway, Joseph, Bruce B. Auster, and Doug Pasternak. "The Bear." *U.S. News & World Report* (February 11, 1991): 32–42.

Hammer, Joshua. "A Mountain of a Man." *Newsweek* (Spring/Summer 1991 Commemorative Edition): 97.

Hewitt, Bill. "America's Desert Leader." *People Weekly* (September 3, 1990): 66–67.

Hewitt, Bill, Linda Kramer, and Mary Huzinec. "Home Is the Hero." *People Weekly* (May 13, 1991): 42–47.

Mackenzie, Richard. "General H. Norman Schwarzkopf." *Insight* (March 18, 1991): 14–16.

Morris, M. E. *H. Norman Schwarzkopf: Road to Triumph*. New York: St. Martin's Press, 1991.

Parrish, Robert D. *Schwarzkopf: An Insider's View of the Commander and His Victory*. New York: Bantam Books, 1991.

Pyle, Richard. *Schwarzkopf: In His Own Words*. New York: Signet, 1991.

Schwarzkopf, Brenda. "Norman Schwarzkopf." *People Weekly* (Spring/Summer 1991 Commemorative Issue): 6–9.

Staff of *People Weekly*. "Stormin' Norman: Born to Win." *People Weekly* (March 11, 1991): 35–39.

Chronology

1934	Born on August 22 near Trenton, New Jersey
1946–50	Lives in Iran, Switzerland, Germany, and Italy
1952	Graduates from Valley Forge Military Academy in Pennsylvania
1956	Graduates from U.S. Military Academy at West Point and begins army career with rank of second lieutenant
1957	After completing Basic Infantry Course at Fort Benning, Georgia, reports to Fort Campbell, Kentucky, for first tour of duty; promoted to first lieutenant in November
1958	Father, H. Norman Schwarzkopf, Sr., dies
1959–61	Schwarzkopf serves in army's Berlin Brigade; promoted to captain in July 1961
1961–62	Attends Infantry Officers' Advanced Course at Fort Benning, Georgia
1962–64	Studies at University of Southern California; receives master's degree in mechanical and aerospace engineering
1964–65	Teaches mechanical engineering at West Point
1965–66	Promoted to major in July 1965; serves as field adviser to South Vietnamese airborne unit during first tour of duty in Vietnam
1966–68	Teaches at West Point; marries Brenda Holsinger in July 1968; promoted to lieutenant colonel in August 1968
1968–69	Attends Command and General Staff College at Fort Leavenworth, Kansas
1969–70	Second tour of duty in Vietnam; serves as battalion commander in Americal Division from December 1969 to July 1970
1970–72	Serves in staff position in Washington, D.C.; daughter Cynthia born in 1970; daughter Jessica born in 1972
1972–73	Attends Army War College in Carlisle, Pennsylvania

1973–74	Serves in army's financial management office at Pentagon
1974–76	Serves as deputy commander of infantry brigade at Fort Richardson, Alaska; promoted to colonel in November 1975
1976–78	Commands infantry brigade at Fort Lewis, Washington; son, Christian, born in 1977; promoted to brigadier general (first star) in August 1978
1978–80	Serves in Pacific Command in Hawaii
1980–82	Serves as assistant commander of infantry division in Europe; promoted to major general (second star) in July 1982
1982–83	Serves in Personnel Office of Pentagon
1983–85	Commands Fort Stewart, Georgia; in October 1983, serves as army adviser during the U.S. invasion of Grenada
1985–86	Serves as army's assistant deputy chief of staff at Pentagon; promoted to lieutenant general (third star) in July 1986
1986–87	Commands infantry corps at Fort Lewis, Washington
1987–88	Serves as army staff officer and member of Military Staff Committee for the United Nations in Washington, D.C.; promoted to full general (fourth star) in November 1988
1988	Receives command of U.S. Central Command in Tampa, Florida
1990	Iraq invades Kuwait on August 1; Schwarzkopf takes command of Operation Desert Shield in Saudi Arabia
1991	Coalition air war against Iraq begins January 17; ground offensive begins February 24; war ends on February 27; Schwarzkopf retires from army on August 31

Index

PICTURE CREDITS

AP/Wide World Photos: pp. 21, 41, 44, 48, 74, 82, 85, 86, 87, 88, 90, 94, 96, 100, 104; Library of Congress: pp. 14, 37, 47, 53; The National Archives: pp. 10, 27, 39, 50; New Jersey State Police Museum: p. 18; Reuters/Bettmann Archive: pp. 91, 97, 98, 99; The United States Military Academy Archives: pp. 30, 34, 36, 38, 42; UPI/Bettmann Archive: pp. 16, 20, 49, 56, 59, 70, 103; U.S. Air Force photo: frontispiece, pp. 72, 84; U.S. Army photo: pp. 15, 66, 73, 106; U.S. Army War College Photo: p. 64; U.S. Navy Photo: p. 77; Valley Forge Military Academy and Junior College, PA: p. 33; Visions Photo Inc.: pp. 23, 24, 54, 62; Maps by Gary Tong: pp. 13, 81, 92, 93

Rebecca Stefoff holds a Ph.D. in English from the University of Philadelphia, where she taught for three years. She is the author of more than 50 nonfiction books for young adults, including numerous biographies of world leaders and contemporary political figures. She has also served as the editor of Chelsea House Publishers' PLACES AND PEOPLES OF THE WORLD and LET'S DISCOVER CANADA series. She lives in Philadelphia.

Vito Perrone is Director of Teacher Education and Chair of Teaching, Curriculum, and Learning Environments at Harvard University. He has previous experience as a public school teacher, a university professor of history, education, and peace studies (University of North Dakota), and as dean of the New School and the Center for Teaching and Learning (both at the University of North Dakota). Dr. Perrone has written extensively about such issues as educational equity, humanities curriculum, progressive education, and evaluation. His most recent books are: *A Letter to Teachers: Reflections on Schooling and the Art of Teaching*; *Enlarging Student Assessment in Schools*; *Working Papers: Reflections on Teachers, Schools, and Communities*; *Visions of Peace*; and *Johanna Knudsen Miller: A Pioneer Teacher.*

WITHDRAWN